PRAYER WORKS

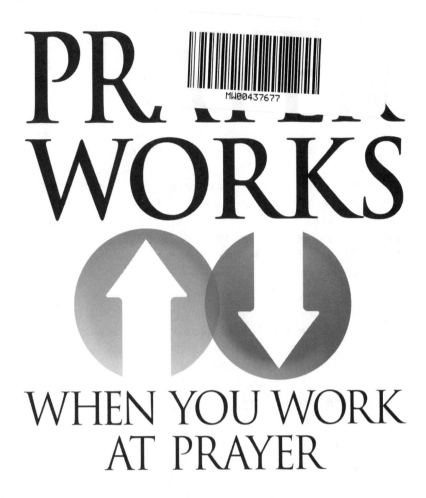

WHEN YOU WORK AT PRAYER

Following Jesus' Example in Prayer

DR. MARK BECTON

publishers
SOLUTION
The Key to Publishing Possibilities

PRAYER WORKS
WHEN YOU WORK AT PRAYER

© 2017 by Dr. Mark Becton

Grove Avenue Baptist Church ~ Dr. Mark Becton, Senior Pastor
8701 Ridge Road • Richmond, Virginia 23229

ISBN: 978-1-937925-22-2 Paperback

Published by:

■publishers
SOLUTION
The Key to Publishing Possibilities

Publishers Solution
P.O. Box 2184 • Forest, VA 24551
www.PublishersSolution.com

Cover & Interior Design by the Publishers Solution Graphic Design Team

CONTENTS

PREFACE

After praying with a friend, he surprised me by asking, "Who taught you to pray?" No one had ever asked me that. The key shapers of my spiritual life were my mom and dad, so I told him they did. Therefore, thank you, Mom and Dad, for not only helping me surrender to Jesus, but learn how to talk with Him.

The more I've thought about my friend's question, others have been influential…particularly my wife, Loree. Married over thirty years, I've now prayed more with her than Mom and Dad. Loree, your love for the Father is evident in the way you often weep and pray. Your faith in Him has strengthened mine, especially when I hear you praying scripture to Him with such gratitude and trust. Your prayers have helped shape mine.

Above all, Thank you Jesus! It's because of who You are that I long to talk with You. You heard me when I was six and surrendered my life to You. You've heard my prayers as a child, adolescent, young parent, and graying man. You've been patient with my flaws and ignorance, and faithful in discipling me. I'm far from spiritiually grown, and yet I know You always listen and answer. And though I don't like some of Your answers, I know You love me. You've taught me how to pray more than anyone else. Jesus, I love You and am so thankful to You.

INTRODUCTION

Well-meaning Christians say, "Prayer is easy. All you have to do is talk with God." Yet if prayer is easy, why do many struggle with it? It's not because people don't believe in prayer. Medical journals record how people who pray heal faster than those who don't. It's not that many don't want to pray or have others pray for them. When I conducted door-to-door surveys, most seemed uncomfortable answering questions regarding spiritual beliefs. But ask, "Is there anything I can pray for you?" smiles appear as they volunteer information.

Though many believe in prayer and want to pray, countless still find it hard. Personally, I've had to work at prayer. I've tried being still with God in the mornings, then felt evenings were better. Some days were a running conversation with God without really making time to be still. I've made prayer a part of my exercise routine. I've joined prayer groups, fasted and prayed, written a prayer journal, and created different types of prayer lists. Some may be so disciplined they can set one time, one place, and utilize one prayer-tool for a lifetime. I wasn't made that way. Yet knowing the importance of prayer, I've worked at it over the years.

This book is for those like me who know the importance of prayer and have to work at it. The best tool I've found is the one Jesus gave in Matthew 6—the Lord's Prayer. Sadly, the Lord's Prayer is often seen as something to repeat instead of a model to use. That's why most recite it mindlessly instead of using it meaningfully as Christ intended. When you look closely at the Lord's Prayer, the familiar statements surface as headings for a prayer list. Those headings are intentionally sequenced by God to produce focused comprehensive prayers.

The first chapter of *Prayer Works* acts as an orientation. Many see prayer more as a routine practiced at church than the product of a relationship with God. As is your relationship with God, so are your prayers. Realizing this, the topics within the Lord's Prayer become more personal. Subsequent chapters encourage picturing God before you pray, praying according to God's will, for your needs, for God to forgive you and to help you forgive others, and for God's protection and strength regarding temptation. The final chapter utilizes the headings in the Lord's Prayer to form a personal prayer list. It inspires praying specifically—for you see specific answers from specific prayers.

We are each fearfully and wonderfully made by God. Therefore, some may want to read this book in one sitting. Others may read a chapter a week working to apply what they've read. It doesn't matter how you use this book. What's important is that you use it. Use it to strengthen your walk with God and God's work through you as you pray.

Chapter 1

PREPARING TO PRAY

L ife is full of prerequisites. Even natural acts like running require them. Consider,

IN ORDER TO RUN, YOU MUST ...

walk before running,
crawl before walking,
and roll before crawling.

Some, however, try skipping a step. My oldest son John Mark was content to roll. Putting toys beyond his reach, Loree and I hoped he'd crawl to them. Unfazed, he smiled, dropped, and rolled to the toy.

My youngest son Lee, on the other hand, did not walk long. He moved his walker like a hovercraft. Though neither of my sons spent the normal time crawling or walking, they spent some time doing so before running.

See the principle? Though created to run, my boys went through steps to do what was natural. According to Genesis 3:8–19, we were created to walk and talk with God. In a passage where God unfolds the consequences for Adam's and Eve's sin, we forget God did this after walking through Eden looking to talk with them.

We were created for intimate conversations with God. Praying should come naturally. But, it doesn't without respecting some important prerequisites. Here are four.

CONFESSION:
Being holy before God before having a relationship with God

Because He is God, God can talk with anyone He chooses. However, His deeper, intimate, and frequent conversations are with those who have a relationship with Him…a relationship requiring holiness on our part. We see this in Genesis 3:8–9. It's God's last conversation with Adam and Eve in Eden.

> *⁸ Then the man and his wife heard the sound of the Lord God walking in the garden at the time of the evening breeze, and they hid themselves from the Lord God among the trees of the garden.⁹ So the Lord God called out to the man and said to him, "Where are you?"*

God creates Adam and Eve sinless. Once they eat the forbidden fruit, God outlines the consequences of their sin

(Genesis 3:10–24). As His final consequence, God removes them from Eden. Adam and Eve are no longer holy before God. Therefore, God no longer walks with them. Their relationship is broken.

Romans 5:12 explains how Adam and Eve's sin affects everyone. All are born sinfully separated from God. Before we can walk and talk with God as He intended, we must return to the condition God demands—holiness. Until then, our prayers are strained because we are talking with God on different channels.

Cable and satellite television removed the unique experience provided by UHF channels. As a child, it frustrated me when VHF and UHF signals competed for the same channel. Though amusing to see Lassie running after Rocky and Bullwinkle, the lack of a clear picture, consistent story, or single message got old.

For the same reasons, our prayers to God become ineffective and frustrating. Because God is holy and we are not, our views and story-lines are on different channels. This makes talking with God challenging at best.

Ultimately, one frequency overcame the other allowing me to focus on one picture and story. When it comes to prayer, God never compromises His holiness to accommodate our sinfulness. Instead, He gives us the opportunity to become holy so we can walk and talk with Him. That opportunity occurs through God's grace and our confession.

1 John 1:9, says, *"If we confess our sins, He is faithful and righteous to forgive us our sins and to cleanse us from*

all unrighteousness." The Greek word for "confess" literally means "to say the same." It means to agree with God.

IN CONFESSION, YOU AGREE WITH GOD

- My sins separate me from You. I have no right to walk and talk with You.
- Jesus, You paid the price for my sin, making my return possible.
- Forgive me of my sins. I want to walk and talk with You all my life.
  *(Such confession involves repentance,
  not just penance.)*

In penance, we do something because we are sorry. Repentance is turning from our sin and surrendering everything to God. Confessing this way, God's grace covers us. It's the Old Testament word "atonement." It means "a covering." Now seeing His grace covering our sin, God sees us as holy. Now on the same channel with God, we walk and talk together. Life changing confession returns us to what we were created to do—pray.

SURRENDER:
*You need a relationship with God
before spending time with God*

Confession represents a major step. Still, you are not ready to run with prayer until you understand surrender.

Romanian pastor Josef T'son translated for American pastor Adrian Rogers as he preached throughout Romania. Traveling to a speaking engagement, Rogers pressed T'son, "Josef, tell me about American Christianity." Hesitant at first, Josef eventually said the key word in American Christianity is "commitment." When Rogers quizzed, "Isn't commitment good?" Josef's answer was both insightful and painful. Josef said,

> No it's not. As a matter of fact, the word *commitment* did not come into great usage in the English language until about the 1960's. In Romania we do not even have a word to translate the English word *commitment*....
>
> When a new word comes into usage, it generally pushes an old word out. I began to study and found the old word that *commitment* replaced. Adrian, the old word that is no longer in vogue in America is the word *surrender*.[1]

Asking Josef to explain the difference between *commitment* and *surrender*, T'son revealed,

> When you make a commitment, you are still in control, no matter how noble the thing you commit to. One can commit to pray, to study the Bible, to give his money, or to commit to automobile

---

[1] Adrian Rogers, *The Incredible Power of Kingdom Authority* (Nashville: Broadman & Holman Publishers, 2002), 60–61.

payments, or to lose weight. Whatever he chooses to do, he *commits* to. But *surrender* is different. If someone holds a gun and asks you to lift your hands in the air as a token of surrender, you don't tell that person what you are committed to. You simply surrender and do as you are told....

Americans love *commitment* because they are still in control. But the key word is *surrender*. We are to be slaves of the Lord Jesus Christ.[2]

What an accurate and humbling description of American Christianity. When it comes to salvation, many choose partial commitment over full surrender. Yet there is no salvation, no real relationship with Jesus, without full surrender (Luke 9:23). Wanting commitment over surrender, we settle for a more comfortable, even manageable relationship with Jesus. But in the end, we miss out on the deep, meaningful (though sometimes painful) life-changing conversations with Him.

Jesus alludes to this in Matthew 6:5, 7, and 8. Before giving us His model prayer, Jesus first offers examples of what prayer is not.

> [5] *"Whenever you pray, you must not be like the hypocrites, because they love to pray standing in the synagogues and on the street corners to be seen by people. I assure you: They've got their reward! ... [7] When you pray, don't babble*

---

[2] Ibid.

*like the idolaters, since they imagine they'll be
heard for their many words. [8] Don't be like them,
because your Father knows the things you need
before you ask Him."*

Prayer is a Relationship, not a Reputation

In verse 5, Jesus points to hypocrites praying in the
synagogues and on the street corners wanting a religious
reputation. They fail to understand prayer overflows from
one's relationship with God...their surrendered life with Him.
As John Bunyan wrote, it is a matter of the heart.

Authorities jailed Bunyan, author of *Pilgrim's Progress*,
for preaching without a license. Twelve years later (1672),
they released him. Resuming his preaching, he sat behind
bars within three years. At some point, Bunyan heard enough
praying in public to write,

In prayer it is better
to have a heart without words
than words without heart.[3]

Prayer is a matter of the heart. It cascades from a surrendered
relationship with God, not a reputation with Him.

Prayer is a Relationship, not a Recitation

In verse 7, Jesus points to pagan prayers. Some Jews in
Jesus' day, like other Eastern beliefs, used prayer-like mantras.

---

[3] John Bunyan, Leadership, Vol. 6, no. 2.

Prophets of Baal did this in 1 Kings 18:26. Dancing around their sacrifice half a day, they chant, *"O Baal, answer us!"* If I spent half a day saying, "Loree, answer me; Loree, answer me; Loree answer me," not only would my wife think I'd lost my mind, but she'd soon lose hers.

Test yourself to see if your prayers are mantras. First, if your prayers at church or before meals sound the same, they are mantras. If you say your prayer without thinking, you are offering a recitation to God and are not praying out of a relationship with Him. It's a mantra.

In Matthew 22:37, Jesus says the greatest commandment is to *"Love the Lord your God with all your heart, with all your soul, and with all your mind."* God not only wants your condition to change covered by His holiness. He also wants your loving surrender to Him to be like His for you (Luke 9:23). Being all in for each other leads to deep heartfelt conversations…not mindless recitations.

TIME:
Spending time with God before building trust in God

Changing your condition (holy) and relationship (surrendered), you may feel closer to God. Still, you are not ready to run in prayer with Him. That comes with time. Knowing how to pray requires spending time praying. You have to spend time with God to truly know Him and build trust in Him. Constant prayer is a must.

Those on surrendered journeys with God know the necessity of prayer. Moses had his tent of meeting with God in Exodus 33. He could have never led Israel to the Promised Land without constantly talking with God as friends. David would have never dropped Goliath and established a nation without his formative time with God as a shepherd boy in Bethlehem's hills. Reminiscing as an old king, he wrote in the 23rd Psalm, *"The Lord is my shepherd, there is nothing I lack."*

Look at Jesus. Jesus started, worked, and completed His ministry utilizing constant prayer. His ministry began after forty days of prayer and fasting (Matthew 4). He then ministered three years spending His early mornings alone with God (Mark 1:35). And on the night before His crucifixion, Jesus prays the most agonizing prayer of His ministry—*"Father, if You are willing, take this cup from me— nevertheless, not My will, but Yours, be done"* (Luke 22:42). Then in Matthew 6:6, Jesus separates His two examples of how not to pray with the following impotant instruction.

> ^{6} *"But when you pray, go into your private room, shut your door, and pray to your Father who is in secret. And your Father who sees in secret will reward you."*

I love the King James Version of this verse. It says, *"when thou prayest, enter into thy closet."* A closet is one room in the house you rarely allow others inside. No one says, "Oh, you must see my closet. Here, step inside with me." Usually, if you are in a closet to get something, you are there alone.

Thus in Matthew 6:6, Jesus says when you pray, get alone with God. Then in Luke 18:1, Jesus encourages when you step from the closet, keep talking with God. If you quit talking with God, it's easy to stop walking with Him.

Joni Erickson Tada explains why constant prayer is so crucial. She says,

Like art, like music, like so many other disciplines,
prayer can only be appreciated
when you actually spend time in it.[4]

Becoming a skilled athlete or artist requires constant practice. Building a strong marriage demands constant communication. If you want to be a strong man or woman of prayer, you must constantly pray.

Here is the priceless return of constant prayer. When you work at prayer, prayer works on you. Constant prayer produces better prayer by creating greater confidence in God—and confidence in God is the final step before running in prayer with Him.

CONFIDENCE:
*You have to build trust in God
before you can run in prayer with God*

The book *The Kneeling Christian* paints a tragic picture of prayer. Worshipers at a shrine in China arrive with their prayers on small pieces of paper. Covering their prayers with

---

[4] Bible Illustrator for Windows, Parsons Technology Inc., 1990-1998.

mud, rolling them into balls, they throw them at an idol. They believe if their prayer balls stick, their prayers will be answered. If they don't, their prayers are rejected.[5]

According to Hebrews 11:6, God does not require you to cover your prayers in mud so they stick and are answered. He does, however, require you to cover them with faith. The verse reads,

> *[6] Now without faith it is impossible to please God, for the one who draws near to Him must believe that He exists and rewards those who seek him.*

Running with God in prayer requires covering your prayers in faith. You must believe God exists and rewards.

Believing that God exists involves more than believing He is out there somewhere. A tree exists but does not have the ability to answer prayer. A prime minister exists but does not have the authority to answer prayer. God alone has both the ability and authority to answer prayer. Therefore when you pray, you are not only to believe that God reigns as King, but you are also to believe that He rewards as Lord.

When you trust the reign and rewards of God, you experience an invaluable confidence in prayer. When praying, you will have:

- …Confidence in the person of God. *You trust His perfect and unchanging character—that*

---

[5] *The Kneeling Christian* (Grand Rapids, Michigan: Zondervan Publishing House, 1971), "Author's Preface."

> *He is "the same yesterday, today and forever."*
> *(Hebrews 13:8)*

- ...Confidence in the plans of God. *You trust His will and way even though you may not understand (Proverbs 3:5–6).*

- ...Confidence in the promises of God. *You quote scripture in prayer not to hold God to His Word, but to thank Him for His promises (Psalm 119:140).*

- ...Confidence in the provisions of God. *You trust that "God will meet all your needs according to his glorious riches in Christ Jesus" (Philippians 4:19).*

When counseling newlyweds, I tell them to protect their trust in each other. In marriage, trust is synonymous with peace. The same is true of your relationship with God. Your degree of faith in God mirrors the degree of confidence you have in prayer. The degree of confidence you have in prayer equals the degree of peace you have in life.

IS IT WORTH IT?

Like running, most think praying is easy and should come naturally. A closer look reveals otherwise. A life of confession, surrender, constant prayer and confidence in God are prerequisites to running with Him in prayer. Hearing all the requirements, you may ask, "Is it worth it?" Let me answer that with the following experience.

For our twentieth anniversary, Loree and I fly to New York City. Of course, we go to see the Empire State Building. To purchase tickets, guides direct us downstairs where we stand in line in a hallway. The line seems short so we wait. When our line turns into a room, we see rows of people waiting to buy tickets from two tellers. But, it's the Empire State Building and we are too excited to turn back.

After purchasing tickets, Loree and I bolt from the room and are pointed to an escalator. We were on our way up. Our smiles disappear entering another hall and line for the metal detector. Thirty minutes later, we walk through without a beep. With the elevators in sight, an attendant says, "To your left, please." It's another room of ropes and lines. Funny two lines ago, Loree and I are now grumpy. Our mood lightens though as we step into the elevator.

The viewing deck of the Empire State Building is on the 86th floor. Our elevator stops on the 80th floor and another attendant instructs, "Step to your right, please." Gritting our teeth, we enter our largest room with the longest line yet. All of us are waiting for the elevator that takes us the last six floors.

Loree and I are now beyond grumpy. After half a day in line, we've seen nothing but halls, rooms, and one elevator. If we knew this up front, we would have skipped it. But finally at the top, the view was breath-taking. We saw the Statue of Liberty and Ellis Island partnered in the distance. The Chrysler Building glistens in the sun as Central Park rests peacefully amidst the skyscrapers.

Earlier when walking the sidewalks of New York City, Loree and I felt pressured by the crowds, noise, and pace. But from our new view, everything seemed calm, pressure-free, almost simple.

Looking back, the journey to the top was harder and longer than expected. Many times Loree and I wanted to turn back. But after reaching the top, seeing what we saw, and experiencing what we experienced, Loree and I would go through it all again because the journey was worth it.

You may think confessing sins to God is too personal, surrendering your life to Him too sacrificial. Though constant prayer is necessary to know God and develop confidence in Him, you may feel it's over the top...especially when all you want to do is pray.

But we're not talking about just any prayer experience. This means reaching the heights with God in prayer. There you see His view of life and so much more. Everything has a different pace and perspective.

Void of such an experience with God you may not think the effort is worth it. But take it from those who have been there... Moses, David, Elijah and more. Doing what is needed to run with God in prayer is more than worth it.

Chapter 2

PRAYING WITH A
BIG PICTURE OF GOD

B orn in 1452, Leonardo da Vinci was a rare man. An expert in multiple disciplines, his genius stands out even today. Most know him for his paintings, such as the *Mona Lisa* and the *Last Supper*. Yet as an engineer, he developed the present canal systems of Milan, Italy. As an inventor, he created a breech-loading cannon. As a geologist, he produced maps of Italy. He also excelled in hydraulics, aeronautics, botany, astronomy, and music.[6]

Hypothetically, if you could learn one discipline from Leonardo da Vinci, what would it be? Though his genius covers many fields, he may be best known for his paintings. You might ask him, "Teach me to paint."

Though rare, Da Vinci's uniqueness falls short of Jesus'. Da Vinci studied the universe Jesus created, and painted

---

[6] *The World Book Encyclopedia* (Field Enterprises Educational Corporation: Chicago, 1965), 39–41.

scenes Jesus lived. Imagine being one of Jesus' disciples... walking and talking with Him three years. You see Him heal, teach, and prophesy. You witness His knowledge of scripture, care for people and wisdom with critics. Yet if you could ask Him to teach you only one discipline, what would it be? The memorable gift in Da Vinci was his ability to paint. Jesus' gift above gifts was how He prayed. That is why His disciples ask Him in Luke 11:1, *"Lord, teach us to pray."*

Jesus answers their request in Luke 11 and in Matthew 6:9–13. We endearingly call it the *Lord's Prayer*. From the greatest man of prayer who ever lived, you have His teachings on prayer. Jesus explains:

> *⁹ "Therefore, you should pray like this:*
> *"'Our Father in heaven,*
> *Your name be honored as holy.*
> *¹⁰ Your kingdom come.*
> *Your will be done*
> *on earth as it is in heaven.*
> *¹¹ Give us today our daily bread.*
> *¹² And forgive us our debts,*
> *as we also have forgiven our debtors.*
> *¹³ And do not bring us into temptation,*
> *but deliver us from the evil one.'"*

In these sixty-two words, Jesus reveals several invaluable lessons on prayer, lessons discussed here and in subsequent chapters.

Jesus first teaches the importance of seeing who you are addressing. In verse 9, Jesus says, *"Therefore, you should pray like this: 'Our Father in heaven, Your name be honored as holy...'"* Jesus opens with three prayer-shaping pictures of God.

GOD THE FATHER:
A Picture of His Care

Jesus begins with a picture of God the Father. It's His cherished picture of God's approachable and faithful care. Together, Mark's and John's Gospels capture it.

Mark's Gospel has Jesus calling God "Father" only six times. Each time He is in the company of His twelve disciples. Through Mark, we know the twelve absorb and understand Jesus' emotions when calling God "Father."

John's record is different. He cites Jesus calling God "Father" around 125 times in a myriad of crowds and settings. John, who is called Jesus' beloved disciple, knew Jesus' intimacy with God the Father. It highlights Jesus' dependence on God. Every day Jesus envisions God's care and strength as His heavenly Father.

Because I had a caring dad, seeing God as a caring Father came easily. My dad was not so fortunate. His dad was an abusive alcoholic. Consequently, Dad seldom talked about his dad. When he did, it was not about his care.

Spending time with men in small groups, I learned Dad's story is tragically common. Many men and women grow up with dads who exhibit little to no form of God's care. So how do you trust God's care if you never experienced it from your dad? How did my dad?

Dad trusted God the Father to give him the care he longed for from his dad. And, God did not disappoint. God became the caring Father Dad never had…the one who lovingly comforted and confronted, and never left even when you blew it.

As a result, Dad became the dad I now want to be. Furthermore, Dad gave me a glimpse of the kind of care I can expect from God the Father. Only a glimpse, mind you, for God's care is deeper, more detailed, and life shaping. God's care is more transforming because it pours from His character, which is forever holy.

That is why Matthew 7:9–11 uses bold colors painting God's parental care. Jesus says,

> [9] *"What man among you, if his son asks for bread, will give him a stone?* [10] *Or if he asks for a fish, will give him a snake?* [11] *If you then, though you are evil, know how to give good gifts to your children, how much more will your Father in heaven give good things to those who ask him!"*

I am far from perfect. Yet, I know the joy in giving gifts to my sons and caring for them. If you and I know that joy as sinful parents, think how much more God enjoys caring for us as the perfect Parent. Therefore, if you ever worry about talking to God about anything, remember, as Jesus' follower…

- God is your heavenly Father. He loves you more than you are loved as a child or love your own children (Matthew 7:9–11).
- God is your heavenly Father. He already knows what you have done, how you hurt, and what you need before you ask (Matthew 6:7–8).
- God is your heavenly Father. No matter what you have done, He cares for you and still wants to fulfill His will through you (Luke 15:1–24).

When praying and calling God "Father," take a breath. Stop and smile. Remember, His love and care is deeper and more reliable than any you've ever experienced. And it's not going away, for it surfaces from His unchanging clout and character.

GOD THE KING:
A Picture of His Clout

I am not an artist, but when painting the *Mona Lisa*, I wonder if Da Vinci did so in layers. Did he first paint the conditions of the day, followed by a landscape under a perfect sky, before finally adding the woman with the simple smile?

Jesus opens His prayer in layers. He begins by envisioning the approachability, care, and loving faithfulness of God the Father. Then, picturing God in heaven, Jesus adds the important layer of God's clout.

Too often, we panic when talking with God. Our tone is an intense mixture of fear, whining and anger. When physically afraid, our adrenalin creates tunnel vision. We focus only on the fear. Panicked over a decision too complicated to resolve, a relationship too broken to mend, a bill too big to pay, we get spiritual tunnel vision. We only see the problem, the small picture, instead of what God may be doing in our problem to reveal His greatness…the big picture.

Picturing "Our Father in heaven" reduces the tension and tunnel vision in our prayers. Futhermore, seeing God's position and power in heaven noticeably changes the tone of our prayers. Here is how. Using the description of heaven found in Revelation 21, imagine yourself hand-delivering your requests to God.

With prayer in hand, you approach heaven awed by the four walls surrounding it. They stand twenty stories tall, made of jasper (v. 18). They are supported by twelve foundations. each comprised of precious gems (v. 19–20). Each wall hosts three gates, each gate cut from a single pearl (v. 10–14, 21). Walking through your gate, you notice it never shuts. There's no need. You are safe in heaven (v. 25–27). You hear different sounds in heaven as well. There are no sirens or sobs from death and pain (v. 3–4). Continuing your walk, you notice the streets and facilities are made of pure transparent gold (v.18). When the glory of God reflects off these, you realize there will never be night in heaven, only day (v. 23).

Overwhelmed with awe, you forget why you are there. Then, you see the prayer in your hand. Reading it, you realize there is nothing on your list God, the King of Heaven, cannot do. With His position and power, He can do anything.

Therefore, consider the following each time you approach God in prayer.

If the prayer in your hand is

- ...for a hurt, look at heaven. You are praying to the God who wipes away every tear. There is no hurt He cannot comfort.
- ...for protection, assurance, or security, look at heaven. You are praying to the God who leaves the doors of heaven open because He is threatened by nothing. Therefore, nothing is so big God cannot protect you from it or walk you through it.
- ...for provisions, look at heaven. Heaven is surrounded by walls of jasper, supported by foundations of gems, lined with buildings made of pure gold. What resource do you need that God cannot provide?
- ...for wisdom or direction, look at heaven. You are praying to the One in charge of heaven. If He can manage all of heaven, I think He can manage what you need.

Thomas Aquinas (1225–1274) wrote *Summa Theologica*. It stands as one of the greatest intellectual achievements of Western civilization. Though containing thirty-eight treatises, three thousand articles, and ten thousand objections, it remains an unfinished work.

Aquinas aspired to create an exhaustive collection of truth. He longed to showcase the truths of God in anthropology, science, ethics, psychology, political theory and theology. Yet on December 6, 1273, Aquinas abruptly stopped writing. While celebrating Mass in St. Thomas' chapel, he had a vision of eternity. Suddenly, he knew all his efforts to describe God fell so woefully short he stopped trying.[7]

Though picturing God in heaven caused Aquinas to stop writing, envisioning God in heaven should encourage you to never stop praying. Aquinas felt God was too big to ever capture in print. However, you should feel God is too big to ever be overwhelmed by your requests. Whatever you ask, God is big enough to meet your need. And however God chooses to meet your need it will be done for His glory alone. That's not only because your heavenly Father has clout, He is also Holy.

HOLY GOD:
A Picture of His Character

In Hebrew, names describe a person's personality, nature, and character. Addressing God in the *Lord's Prayer*, Jesus says, *"Our Father in heaven, hallowed be your name..."(NIV)*. Jesus calls His Father "Hallowed." Hallowed is the verb form of the noun "holy." "Holy" means to be separate or different.

---

7 Don McCullough, "Reasons to Fear Easter," Preaching Today, Tape No. 116.

God inspires biblical writers to use over 85 names to describe Him.[8] The name used most (over 6,500 times) is Yahweh. It means "I Am Who I Am." When praying, we must not address God the way we want Him to be...agreeing with everything we think and feel. As Yahweh, He reminds us "I have my own view and will. I Am Who I Am." Knowing our nature to be self-absorbed, Jesus stresses the importance of opening each prayer picturing God's character...seeing Him as forever holy.

In prayer, we correctly expect an all-knowing God to perfectly understand us and our requests. However, we forget He views our lives and prayers through a different lens—holiness. Viewing everything through His holiness, God purposely answers prayer to reveal what makes Him different (holy) from us. Once we remove our self-centered lenses and see God's holy ways, our jaws drop over His greatness. This dramatically affects how we now view our lives and our prayers. Just ask Isaiah.

In Isaiah 6, Isaiah enters the temple broken over godly King Uzziah's death. There, God reveals His holiness to Isaiah. The experience changes everything about him. Seeing God's holiness, Isaiah immediately sees, confesses and repents of his sin (Isaiah 6:1-7).

Picturing God's holiness in prayer does the same today. We cannot stay in God's presence with unconfessed sin. His holiness surfaces it until we repent and confess it. Doing so removes

---

[8] Tony Evans, *Praying Through the Names of God* (Eugene, Oregon: Harvest House Publishers, 2014), 11.

our self-centered lens. We now see our lives and circumstances with holy eyes as God does. Doing so changes our priorities, purpose, and plans…just as it did Isaiah's (Isaiah 6:8-10).

That does not mean we do not get frustrated when God doesn't answer every prayer when or the way we want. However, in time we learn to trust His different (holy) perspective. We even become thankful knowing His character never changes. In a world where views and values change with the weather, God's do not (Hebrews 13:8). Praise God, His character remains the same. He is forever holy.

THE BIG PICTURE OF GOD AND PRAYER

You may ask, "Why is it important to open prayer with a big picture of God? Paul's experience in Athens explains what happens when failing to pray with a big picture of God.

LESSON #1
Without a Big Picture of God,
Your Prayers Are Diluted.

In Acts 17, Paul waits in Athens to join his friends, Timothy and Silas. Verses 16–17 record what he sees:

> *16 While Paul was waiting for them in Athens, his spirit was troubled within him when he saw that the city was full of idols. 17 So he reasoned in the synagogue with the Jews and with those who worshiped God in the marketplace every day with those who happened to be there.*

Seeing the idols, Paul discovers Athens' reputation is true. People said "it was easier to meet a god than a man in Athens."[9] With so many gods vying for their attention, Athenians couldn't focus on one god to offer a legitimate prayer.

Rushing into prayer without a big picture of God, you risk letting other gods dilute it. The god of school or career comes to mind because of impossible deadlines. The god of family grabs your attention because their demands are more than you can fulfill. The god of finances appears with each bill and your concerns over paying it. Then, the god of the calendar screams there is no more of you left to give.

Beginning your prayer with all this on your mind, how can you truly talk with God? Furthermore, how will you see God as bigger than your needs if all you see are your needs and never God?

Seeing God first shrinks your needs and strengthens your prayer. Seeing your needs first strengthens your worries and weakens your prayer. Open your prayer with a big picture of God.

LESSON #2
Without a Big Picture of God, Your Prayers Are Distorted.

Paul understands something else in Athens. He addresses it in verses 22–23:

---

[9] William Barclay, *The Acts of the Apostles* (Philadelphia: The Westminster Press, 1976), 30.

---

²² Then Paul stood in the middle of the Areopagus and said: "Men of Athens! I see that you are extremely religious in every respect. ²³ For as I was passing through and observing the objects of your worship, I even found an altar on which was inscribed: TO AN UNKNOWN GOD. Therefore, what you worship in ignorance, this I proclaim to you."

Athens enshrined more idols than other Greek cities. Just in case they missed one, they erected an idol "To An Unknown God." This proves an ageless point—even religious people can pray to a god they do not know. Sadly, many like it that way.

If you truly don't know God, His likes and dislikes, His standards and ways, then you make them what you want. If you are praying to the god you want instead of to the God that is (Yahweh—I Am Who I Am), your prayers are distorted. You need to begin with a big, clear, and accurate picture of God if your prayers are to be effective, not distorted.

Clarity in prayer comes with more time in God's Word, in prayer, and even in suffering (Philippians 3:10–11) Paul learned, as many have, pain is the classroom where God has our attention. There, He reveals endearing and securing truths about Himself—truths we would have never known outside His school of suffering.

LESSON #3
With a Big Picture of God,
Your Prayers Are Dynamic.

The benefits of opening prayer with a big picture of God appear in an old Roman tale. As an emperor and his troops return home from a victory, Roman soldiers line the streets holding back the cheering crowds. A platform near the street houses the empress and her children. As the emperor's chariot approaches, his youngest son darts from the platform.

The hip-high boy presses through the crowd only to be stopped by the immovable arm of a soldier. He barks, "Stop there, boy. Don't you know who is in that chariot? That is the emperor. You can't run to him." The young heir to the empire laughs telling the soldier, "He may be your emperor, but that man in the chariot is my father."[10]

Consider what happens when opening your prayer with a big picture of God. All the treasures of Rome, all the treasures of the world, cannot compare to the treasures of heaven where God the King sits on His throne. There is nothing you ask He cannot provide, nothing you request He cannot do. God has that kind of clout. Yet, God's kingly clout is matched by His holy character. Though He can give you anything you ask and do everything you request, He answers prayer to display His glory...for His character is holy. Above all, God wants you to look upon Him with the eyes of a loving child who says,

---

[10] William Barclay, *The Gospel of Matthew* (Philadelphia: The Westminster Press, 1976), 203.

I know you are God the King
  with all the clout of heaven.
I know you are God, and are Holy,
  with a character pure and strong.
But above all, I know the one on the throne
  is God, my Father;
Who lets me run to Him
  any time at all.

What a picture of God! Now you are ready to pray.

Chapter 3

PRAYING FOR GOD'S KINGDOM

SEEING THE LAYERS

Looking at a painting over time causes you either to marvel at or miss details. The same can happen with the Lord's Prayer. Some, like me, have been so familiar with the Lord's Prayer we miss an important detail. It is layered. Like building blocks, each request becomes the foundation for the next. For example, only by picturing God first will His kingdom trump our panic.

When overwhelmed by need (the potential loss of job, love. health, anything) or opportunity (the potential of college acceptance, job promotion, getting married, starting a family, and more), we panic and run to God. Yet, Jesus instructs us not to open with panic. Instead, stop, breathe, and consider the One you are addressing.

Remember, God adopted you. You are His and all He is and has is yours (Romans 8:12-17). He is your caring, ever-present, perfect Father. Then try to envision how heaven sees and celebrates God (Revelation 4–5). What makes God worshipped in heaven is what you know to be true of Him on earth. God is holy. We rest in His perfect unchanging character.

Unless you are disobeying God, the natural reflex of seeing Him is a hunger to see Him more. Exodus 33:11 says Moses talks face to face with God as friends. It's not that they talked nose to nose. "Face to face" describes an intimate conversation. Such intimacy drives Moses to ask God in verse 18, *"Please, let me see your glory."* Moses aches to see more of God. God essentially tells him in verses 19–23, "I'll let you see as much as you can handle."[11]

For Jesus' followers, this hunger to see God more leads to spending more time with Him in prayer. Spending more time with God in prayer transforms you. You start talking like the One you frequently talk with. That means you begin praying more like Jesus. As you pray more like Jesus, you find yourself praying for what God wants (His kingdom) more than what you want (your panic/daily bread). You see this in Matthew 6:9–10,

---

[11] A great read on Moses' experience with God in Exodus 32–33 is Thomas D. Elliff, *The Pathway to God's Presence* (Nashville, Tennessee: Broadman Press, 1990). Another benefit of picturing God in prayer is it calms our your panics. Spotlighting your need or opportunity causes its shadow to terrorize you. We all know how backlighting something small exaggerates its size. Shift the spotlight from your panic to God shows the true size of your need or opportunity. Thus as the shadow shrinks, so does your panic.

> [9] *"Therefore, you should pray like this:*
> *"'Our Father in heaven,*
> *Your name be honored as holy.*
> [10] *Your kingdom come.*
> *Your will be done*
> *on earth as it is in heaven.'"*

See how the layers work. The step of picturing of God in prayer becomes the stepping stone to praying "Your kingdom come." It re-focuses our panicked prayers into Kingdom prayers. And consistently praying Kingdom prayers allows us to be a part of what God is doing.

As a child, I liked it when Dad involved me in something important to him. I was invited into Dad's world and entrusted with something bigger than me. It was exciting, affirming, stretching and growing for me.

The same happens in this natural progression of prayer. Seeing God, we not only want to see Him more, but we also want be a part of what He's doing. In verse 10, Jesus identifies God's singular focus. He is passionate about His kingdom. This chapter focuses on what it means to be a part of God's work when praying "Your Kingdom come." Next chapter we'll learn to pray "Your will be done"—what it takes to get the work done.

"YOUR KINGDOM COME"
The Aim

George Buttrick says when praying "Your kingdom

come," you ask God to conduct a major operation.[12] I'd rather say, you're asking to be involved in what God is doing. As Henry Blackaby teaches, God is always at work. Our job is to see it and join Him. It helps, however, to know what God's kingdom work looks like. According to the way "kingdom" is used in the New Testament, God's kingdom work moves in three waves.

Wave #1: "Your Kingdom Come" – Within Me

The Greek word for "kingdom" refers to sovereignty, not territory.[13] The empires of Alexander, Julius Caesar, and Napoleon Bonaparte appear on maps while the kingdom of God is seen in hearts. Those who see Jesus as God, surrender to Him as Savior, love and obey Him as Lord make up the kingdom of God.

When you pray "Your kingdom come," you are first praying for God's kingdom to spread within you. Jesus says, in Luke 17:20–21,

---

[12] https://books.google.com/books?id=mFtMAwAAQBAJ&pg
=PT122&lpg=PT122&dq=george+buttrick+quotes+praying+th
y+kingdom+come&source=bl&ots=RMheSguYlR&sig=gNwr1
yYQEVA-jKYIkwcEHVaOtTk&hl=en&sa=X&ved=0ahUKEwj
It7azhZrTAhUq2IMKHfvKAJAQ6AEIGjAA#v=onepage&q=george%20
buttrick%20quotes%20praying%20thy%20kingdom%20come&f=false.

[13] James Strong, *The Exhaustive Concordance of the Bible* (McLean, Virginia: MacDonald Publishing Company, nd), 569–570. Strong shows "basileia" as the only word tranlsated in the New Testatment as "kingdom." Vine's Expository Dictionary of Biblical Words, Copyright © 1985, Thomas Nelson Publishers, explains that "basileia "is primarily an abstract noun, denoting 'sovereignty, royal power, dominion....'"

> *²⁰ Now when He was asked by the Pharisees when the kingdom of God would come, He answered them and said, "The kingdom of God does not come with observation; ²¹ nor will they say, 'See here!' or 'See there!' For indeed, the kingdom of God is within you."* NKJV

Jesus says the kingdom of God is not about measurables. Many point to large crowds and mass baptisms as signs of the spread of the kingdom of God. Yet, two or three generations removed from the experience and the culture is no different. Many times it's worse.

Therefore, Jesus stresses the first place to look for the spread of God's kingdom is within His followers. Upon surrendering your life to Jesus, you become a part of God's kingdom because the life of the King now lives within you. There should be evidence of His reign by the way you submit to His authority in all matters of life.

Praying, "Your kingdom come," helps us assess, "How much of my life does Jesus still rule?" You once promised Him all of your life or He would not have entered. How much of your promise have you kept?

At salvation, we surrender to God as Lord. Yet, as His spirit marches through us, we are tempted to close off territories to Him. For us to pray "Your kingdom come," all territories of our life must remain open to God.

Galatians 5:19–21 lists the acts of our sinful nature. These represent territories often closed to God. Though most are self-explanatory, I'll clarify a few.

Acts of the Sinful Nature Include:

sexual immorality
fits of rage
impurity (an unsifted life)
selfish ambition
debauchery (ready for any pleasure)
dissensions (a wedge in relationships)
idolatry (choosing anything over God)
factions
witchcraft
envy (jealousy with a grudge)
hatred
drunkenness
discord (quarrellings)
orgies
jealousy and the like (other ungodly characteristics)

Then in verse 21, God warns:

[21] ...I tell you in advance—as I told you before— that those who practice such things will not inherit the kingdom of God.

Therefore, when praying "Your kingdom come," ask God to show you any un-surrendered territories in your life. Ask Him to help you re-surrender all territories to Him. To better use you in the battle around you, God must win the war within you. Pray "May Your kingdom come within me."

Wave #2: "Your Kingdom Come" – Through Me

As God conquers more within you, He conquers more through you. That's why praying "Your kingdom come" asks for God's kingdom to spread both within you and through you. Jesus explains this in Luke 13:18–21.

> *[18] He said, therefore, "What is the kingdom of God like, and what can I compare it to? [19] It's like a mustard seed that a man took and sowed in his garden. It grew and became a tree, and the birds of the sky nested in its branches."*
> *[20] Again He said, "What can I compare the kingdom of God to? [21] It's like yeast that a woman took and mixed into 50 pounds of flour until it spread through the entire mixture."*

Jesus' two examples describe small items that expand. In a lost world, most followers feel small. Yet, the book of Acts is full of inspiring examples of God's kingdom spreading through believers.

In Acts 1–2, 120 pray ten days seeing 3,000 saved at the Feast of Pentecost. Six months later, by Acts 6, God's kingdom has spread to 8,000, but they are all in Jerusalem. In Acts 8, God uses Philip to spread His kingdom to Samaria and Ethiopia. In Acts 9, God commissions Paul to spread it among the Gentiles. The book of Acts reads as a journal of God's kingdom expanding through believers praying and following God's lead in spreading the gospel.

Centuries later, God's kingdom continued advancing through tireless prayer. A drunken law student, Martin Luther, surrenders to Jesus and prays three hours a day and sees Germany spiritually reformed. The fifteenth of nineteen children, John Wesley could have been hidden in his own family. Praying two hours a day, he follows God's lead in changing England. Some could have overlooked the four-feet-three-inch woman from Virginia. However, Lottie Moon's small life and big prayers impacted more than her beloved China. Inspired by Moon, people have given billions of dollars toward spreading the kingdom of God.

In my lifetime, you have George McCluskey. George prays daily from 11:00 a.m. to noon for his children, grandchildren and great-grandchildren. As a result his two daughters marry ministers. His four granddaughters marry ministers and his one grandson becomes a pastor. His first two great-grandchildren are boys. As you would guess, one becomes a pastor. The other, however, pursues his interest in psychology earning his doctorate. Before you think this one great-grandson missed God's call, think again. He is prolific author and founder of Focus on the Family, James Dobson.[14]

Consider how the kingdom of God spread through George McCluskey. It spread to numerous lives spanning four generations all because he was willing to pray, "Your kingdom come through me."

Thus, it is important to remember that...

---

[14] Steve Farrar, *Point Man* (Portland, Oregon: Multnomah Books, 1990), 154–55.

- when you pray *"Your kingdom come within me,"* you are praying for your relationship with God. You want to be sure He is Lord of all territories of your life.

- when you pray *"Your kingdom come through me,"* you are praying for your responsibility to God. God is as passionate to have a relationship with others as He is passionate about His relationship with you.

- when you pray *"Your kingdom come,"* you are praying to keep your relationship with God and your responsibility to God in balance. Some by nature will want to soak up time with God without serving Him, while others will want to serve Him without spending time with Him. God wants both.

These first two waves of the kingdom of God make your prayers more earnest. The third wave, however, makes your prayers more urgent.

Wave #3: "Your Kingdom Come" – Once and For All

As already said, the word "kingdom" refers to a reign, not a region; to God's sovereignty, not territory. However, the word "come" adds something important. The Greek grammar conveys a one-time act with ongoing implications. Some see it referring to the ultimate consummation of the kingdom of God explained in 1 Thessalonians 4:16–17.

[16] For the Lord Himself will descend from heaven with a shout, with the archangel's voice and with the trumpet of God, and the dead in Christ will rise first. [17] Then we who are still alive will be caught up together with them in the clouds to meet the Lord in the air and so we will always be with the Lord.

The ultimate aim of the kingdom of God points to this grand moment. Therefore, praying "Your kingdom come" requires praying for your surrender, your service, and Jesus' return.

Praying for Jesus' second coming adds urgency to our surrender and service to Jesus. Our lifetime is a breath in the timeline of God. We don't have time to play church or be disctracted from our surrender to Jesus. Prayer enables us to faithfully serve Jesus till He says, "Time's up!"

You hear that sense of urgency in "A Knight's Prayer." Established in 907 A. D., Chester Cathedral remains the most complete medieval monastic complex still standing in Great Britain. Inscribed on a wall you find this prayer:

My Lord, I am ready on the threshold of this new day to go forth armed with thy power, seeking adventure on the high road, to right wrong, to overcome evil, to suffer wounds and endure pain if need be, but in all things to serve thee bravely, faithfully, joyfully, that at the end of the day's labor, kneeling for thy blessing, thou mayst find no blot upon my shield.[15]

---

[15] Edythe Draper, *Draper's Book of Quotations for the Christian World* (Wheaton: Tyndale House Publishers, Inc., 1992). Entries 9087–9088.

May all praying "Your kingdom come" exhibit the same earnest urgency as this knight. May we earnestly surrender all so God's kingdom spreads fully within us, urgently through us, until Jesus returns. And on that day may we long to stand before Him fulfilled—with no blot on our shield. May this be on our minds each time we pray, "Your kingdom come."

Chapter 4

PRAYING FOR GOD'S WILL

> [9] *"Therefore, you should pray like this:*
> *"'Our Father in heaven,*
> *Your name be honored as holy.*
> [10] *Your kingdom come.*
> *Your will be done*
> *on earth as it is in heaven.'"*
> *– Matthew 6:9–10*

Heading Russia's Communist Party in the 1950s and 60s, Nikita Khrushchev said, "Call it what you will, incentives are the only way to make people work harder."[16] If Khrushchev is right, what incentives make us work harder at prayer? More specifically, what motivates us to pray, "Your will be done"?

---

[16] Joe Griffith, *Speaker's Library of Business Stories, Anecdotes and Humor* (Paramus, New Jersey: Prentice Hall, 1990), 225.

SIX INCENTIVES FOR PRAYING
"Your Will Be Done"

Realizing we are different and driven by different motivations, here are six incentives to pray "Your will be done."

Incentive #1
AN EXTREME EXPERIENCE:
"Seeing the Fullness of God"

If driven to experience what most avoid, praying "Your will be done" is for you. According to Matthew 6:9, praying "Your will be done" requires seeking the fullness of a caring, powerful and holy God. Seeking God's fullness, willing to go through painful change so that you want what He wants, is not for the timid. Praying "Your will be done" is for those open for an extreme experience with God.

Incentive #2
A WORTHY CAUSE:
"Fulfilling the Kingdom of God"

If causes inspire you, then you will be obsessed with praying, "Your will be done." God's cause is to be glorified as His Kingdom comes within you, through you, and ultimately to all who surrendered to Him. But Jesus knows His Kingdom will not fully come until His will is fully done. An aim is not achieved without actions, and a cause not completed without surrender. If you long for God's Kingdom to come, you will be moved to pray "Your will be done."

Incentive #3
A CLOSE RELATIONSHIP:
"Included in the Family of God"

While some yearn for extreme experiences or worthy causes, relationships drive others. If fulfilled by walking, talking, and working with those you love, then you will want to pray "Your will be done." Jesus promises in Matthew 12:50, *"For whoever does the will of my Father in heaven, that person is my brother and sister and mother."* Fulfilling God's will gives you a tight relationship with others longing to do the same, and rewards each of you with greater intimacy with God.

Incentive #4
COMPLETE SATISFACTION:
"Enjoying the Food of God"

If you are looking for fulfillment, praying "Your will be done" offers indescribable satisfaction. After meeting the needs of a woman at a well, Jesus overflows in John 4:34, *"My food is to do the will of Him who sent Me and to finish His work."* Doing God's will was Jesus' food. It left Him completely satisfied.

Finding the one food that satisfies all is humanly impossible. Growing up, our boys had selective tastes. One liked corn only on the cob. The other liked corn in any form except on the cob. The one vegetable both agreed on was potatoes, but only if they were baked, mashed, or fried.

Though satisfying everyone's tastes is humanly impossible, it is not spiritually. Praying "Your will be done" and doing God's will becomes your favorite food. It satisfies completely.

Incentive #5
LASTING ACCOMPLISHMENTS:
"Bearing the Fruit of God"

Leaving a legacy fuels many. The longest legacies and greatest accomplishments come by praying "Your will be done." Jesus said in John 15:16, *"You did not choose Me, but I chose you. I appointed you to go out and produce fruit and that your fruit should remain."* As a believer, God chose you to be involved in producing His fruit. He appointed you to accomplish things for His kingdom and glory. But, you'll never see His fruit nor accomplish those feats without praying, "Your will be done."

Incentive #6
ETERNAL SECURITY:
"Confident in your Future with God"

Finally, praying "Thy will be done" has a universal incentive. George Bernard Shaw said, "The statistics on death are quite impressive. One out of one people dies."[17] Everyone wants to go to heaven when they die. Praying "Your will be done" and then doing God's will secures your future with God. In Matthew 7:21 Jesus says, *"Not everyone who says to Me, 'Lord, Lord!' will enter the kingdom of heaven, but only the one who does the will of My Father in heaven."* If you want to be confident in your future with God, pray "Your will be done" and do it.

---

[17] http://www.scriptureunion.org.uk/uploads/wordlight/resources/Spring%20 9%20resource%20sheet%20life%20and%20death.pdf

Jesus announces each of these incentives. Yet, many fail to take advantage of them by praying, "Your will be done." It could be most are like John. John was part of a small business creating a pension plan. For the plan to go into affect, everyone had to sign on and contribute. All had but John. After constant pleas from other workers, the president of the company called John to his office. He said, "John, here are the papers for the new pension plan and a pen. Sign them or you're fired." Agreeably, John said, "Sure" and signed them. Confused, the boss asked, "John, why did you wait till now to sign?" John answered diplomatically, "Nobody explained it to me as clearly as you."[18]

Let me make this as clear as John's boss. If you sign on and earnestly pray "Your will be done," you will receive all the benefits mentioned above. However, if you fail to sincerely pray and strive for God's will to be done, you receive none of them. Hopefully, you will be like John and say, "Nobody has explained this to me as clearly as you. Where do I sign on? How do I pray, 'Your will be done'?"

WHAT TO PRAY WHEN PRAYING
"Your Will Be Done"

Before praying God's will be done, it's important to discern God's will. Volumes line shelves on the subject. For the sake of time, here is a simple principle for discerning God's will: "listen and look for consistency."

---

[18] Griffith, 227.

God speaks to us multiple ways. The most reliable include speaking through His Word, answered prayer, and godly people. Since it is impossible for God to lie (Num. 23:19; 1 Cor. 14:33; Titus 1:2; Heb. 6:12–18), when these three agree, you have likely discerned God's will.

Furthermore, if you want to learn how to pray for God's will, listen to those who do it faithfully. Their prayers teach you what to pray. Of course the best to hear pray is Jesus.

The Bible records two unique examples of Jesus in prayer. The one in Matthew 6 is Jesus' model prayer. Here, Jesus teaches us how to pray. The other surfaces in John 17. As Jesus prays alone to God, we learn what to pray. According to Jesus' prayer, there are four requests when praying, "Your will be done."

Pray for God's Greatness

Jesus opens His prayer in John 17 praying for God's greatness. Verse 1 reads, *"Father, the hour has come. Glorify your Son so that the Son may glorify you."* Jesus uses the word "glory" eight times in His prayer. The New Testament concept of "glory" refers to a personal experience. You personally experience the greatness of God. In Old Testament Hebrew, "glory" points to the impressive acts and events of God. These are acts and events displaying God's greatness.

Focusing on the glory of God, Jesus raises the bar of prayer. Praying for God's will, you ask God to do what only God can do. To see if you are praying for God's will to be done and His greatness seen, ask yourself these questions.

- If God answered my prayer, would I be blown away by His greatness?
- If God answered my prayer, would even the unsaved have to acknowledge His greatness?
- Do my prayers give God the best opportunity to reveal His greatness—for His benefit, not mine?

When praying for God's will to be done, make a big request of a big God. Give Him the best opportunity to reveal His greatness. However, make sure your prayer is to fulfill God's will, not yours. Let it showcase God's greatness, not yours. Follow Habakkuk's lead when he prays in Habakkuk 3:2, *"LORD, I stand in awe of Your deeds. Revive Your work in these years; make it known in these years."* Pray "Your will be done," wanting a great God to reveal His greatness.

Pray for God's Protection

If you are willing to pray for God's greatness, Jesus knows you will have to pray for God's protection. It's a must when praying for God's will, as seen in Jesus' prayer.

Twice in John 17 Jesus prays for God to protect His disciples. First in verses 11–12, and then again in verse 15. Jesus prays, *"My prayer is not that you take them out of the world but that you protect them from the evil one."* Jesus is praying for the protection of His followers. He knows what Satan, "the evil one," will do.

Genesis 3:15 represents the first prophetic announcement about Jesus. After Satan deceives Adam and Eve, God tells him Jesus *"...will crush your head, and you will strike his heel."* God promises Satan Jesus will come and destroy him.

Jesus' prayer in John 17 occurs on the eve of His crucifixion. His resurrection signals the imminent destruction of Satan. Knowing this was about to happen and that Satan will look for one last opportunity to strike back, Jesus prays for the protection of His disciples.

In 1999, the *New England Journal of Medicine* published a study from two toxicologists in Phoenix, Arizona. They learned that in a ten-month period, fifteen percent of those admitted for a snake bite had been bitten by a dead snake. Apparently, a snake's reflexes can continue one hour after its head has been cut off. Though the snake has been decapitated, by pure reflexes it still strikes.[19]

The same is true of Satan. Though his fate is sealed, he looks for one last opportunity to strike. Since he cannot affect your salvation as a believer, he strikes at your effectiveness as a follower. Here is how he strikes.

Satan strikes at your...

- Purity—*making you too spiritually sick to pray and serve.*
- Priorities—*making you too physically busy to pray and serve.*
- Perspective—*making you too emotionally apathetic or spiritually compromised to pray and serve.*

---

[19] Raymond McHenry, *McHenry's Stories for the Soul* (Peabody, Massachusetts: Hendrickson Publishers, 2001), 254–55.

Therefore, when you pray "Your will be done," faithfully pray for your protection. Pray your purity is strong, priorities straight, and perspectives right. Pray for your protection so you'll continue praying for God's will to be done and that you'll be strong enough to do what He asks.

Pray for Your Transformation

The first two requests in Jesus' prayer involve God. Jesus prays for God's greatness and protection. The remaining two requests involve us. Jesus prays for our transformation and our oneness.

Praying both "Your kingdom come" and "Your will be done" mandates transformation. When praying "Your kingdom come," you are praying for God's kingdom to come within you, through you, and ultimately for all who believe. God's kingdom can't spread within you without making more room for Him. Jesus prays this in John 17:16–17. Thinking of His disciples, He prays,

> *[16] "They are not of the world, even as I am not of the world. [17] Sanctify them by the truth; Your word is truth."*

The word "sanctify" literally means "to make holy." With this in mind, I often pray for God's Spirit to fill me and press on every sin until I confess and repent those sins making more room for Him to fill me.

Scripture is another tool God uses to empty us of sin and fill us with Him. Jesus prays in verse 17, *"Sanctify them by the truth; your word is truth.* " Pray God's Word pours through you making the changes God desires.

Many boast of reading through the Bible, or attending church. Sanctification is not how much you read, but how God changes you. It is not sitting in church, but God's Spirit filling you. Thus praying "Your will be done" involves prayers of transformation.

Specifically,

- Pray to be more emptied of sin and more full of Him (Galatians 2:20).
- Pray to become the man or woman God planned when He fashioned you in the womb (Psalm 139).
- Pray when others see you, they see Jesus (Philippians 3:10–11).

The importance of transformation cannot be overstated. The more transformed you are the more informed you are about God's will. The more you know God's will, the more you pray, "Your will be done."

Pray for Your Oneness

The last request Jesus prays is for your oneness. In John 17:20–21, Jesus prays,

> [20] *"I pray not only for these, but also for those who will believe in Me through their message.* [21] *May they all be one, as You, Father, are in Me*

and I am in You. May they also be in Us, so the world may believe You sent Me."

Here, Jesus prays for the breadth and depth of your oneness with Him and others. God preserves this request in scripture knowing our need to constantly pray it.

Praying for the breadth of your oneness with God means praying for others' salvation. Jesus prays in verse 20, *"I pray not only for these, but also for those who will believe in Me through their message."* Jesus expects you to live the gospel and guide those He is drawing. This should always be in your mind and prayers.

As more are added to God's family, you pray for oneness within the family. Jesus' prayer in verse 21 is that all who are saved *"may...be one, Father, as You, Father, are in Me and I am in You. May they also be in Us, so the world may believe You sent Me."* Now, Jesus prays for the depth of your oneness.

After three decades as a pastor, I have seen episodes in churches I long to forget. I've witnessed long-time Christians fearful of the enthusiasm of new believers. I have also watched new believers criticize the wisdom of more mature followers. Embarrassed by the way Christians talked to each other and about each other, I hoped those looking for Jesus were not looking at my church during these episodes. That is why Jesus' prayer should also be your prayer. Pray...

- that your oneness with believers grows deeper, and that your relationship with other believers proves Jesus is real.

- that your oneness as a believer grows broader, and that others become one with Jesus and you as you live and talk about Him.

If it was important for Jesus to pray these prayers, it should be important for us to pray them as well.

WHAT TO EXPECT WHEN PRAYING
"Your Will Be Done"

When you pray, expect more than you think. During a trip to Stockholm, Sweden, Eduardo Sierra walks into an old church to pray. Inside rests a lone casket with no flowers, no family, and a single condolence book beside it. After praying several minutes for the family of the deceased, he's the first to sign the book.

Weeks later, Eduardo receives a call from the Swedish capital informing him he is now a millionaire. Apparently, the man in the casket was a seventy-three-year-old real estate dealer without any family. It was in his will that whoever came and prayed for him inherited everything he had.[20] Eduardo was the only one who came and prayed.

If I told you praying "Your will be done" would make you a millionaire, would you do it? Most likely you would. God does not offer a million dollars for your prayer. Still, you receive items far more valuable. Particularly when praying "Your will be done,"

---

[20] Ibid, 221–222.

When you pray "Your will be done"

1. You will receive the extreme experience of seeing the fullness of God.
2. You will engage in the fulfilling cause of God's Kingdom.
3. You will enjoy a close relationship with God and those in His family.
4. You will experience the satisfaction of doing God's will.
5. You will be a part of God producing His lasting fruit.
6. You will be assured of your salvation and your future with God.
7. You will see and show others God's greatness.
8. You will have God's protection from Satan's snake bites.
9. You will undergo transformation in becoming more like God.
10. You will see the addition of other believers and become more one with them and God.

These ten items are part of God's will. Unlike the deceased Swede, God is not dead. He personally gives these priceless gifts to all who regularly and sincerely pray, "Your will be done."

Chapter 5

PRAYING FOR DAILY BREAD

⁹ *"Therefore, you should pray like this:*
"'Our Father in heaven,
Your name be honored as holy,
¹⁰ *Your kingdom come.*
Your will be done
on earth as it is in heaven.
¹¹ *Give us today our daily bread.*
¹² *And forgive us our debts,*
as we also have forgiven our debtors.
¹³ *And do not bring us into temptation,*
but deliver us from the evil one.'"
— Matthew 6:9–13

As a dad hands out bus fares to his family, all receive their fare except four-year-old Nina. Feeling left out, she asks her mother, "What about me?!" Her mother explains, "Nina, you're free." Confused, Nina protests, "No, I'm not, Mommy! I'm four!"[21]

Jesus first teaches us to pray thinking of God, then His Kingdom and will. Feeling like Nina, we ask God, "What about me? When do I get to tell You about my needs?" I imagine Jesus spreading a smile saying, "Be patient. I'm getting to you."

An overview of the Lord's Prayer reveals five focuses of prayer. Remember, the more pure the effort, the more effective the prayer. Therefore, according to Matthew 6:9–13,

The Lord's Prayer involves praying for…

- The Right Perspective—*Seeing the fullness of God* (v. 9)
- The Right Priorities—*Fulfilling the kingdom and will of God* (v. 10)
- The Right Provisions —*Asking God to meet your daily needs* (v. 11)
- The Right Relationships—*Maintaining a godly relationship with God and others* (v. 12)
- The Right Protection—*Following God's leadership relying on His protection* (v. 13)

Insightfully, God does not allow us to pray for our provisions until our perspective and priorities are right. This

---

[21] Judith Lee and Gretchyn Bailey, "Myopia (Nearsightedness)" http://www.allaboutvision.com/conditions/myopia.html.

helps us focus on our needs instead of wants. Furthermore, God makes sure our needs are met so we can focus on our relationships and His leadership. Thus, at the heart of the Lord's Prayer, we pray, *"Give us today our daily bread."* God does not take this request lightly and neither should we.

EVERY DAY IS A GIFT
"GIVE us today..."

Praying, *"Give us today our daily bread,"* explodes with intensity. The Greek word "give" is punched as an imperative command. "Give us today" when prayed personally becomes "Give me today!" It sounds like Caleb's request in Joshua 14:12. Waiting forty years to claim his section of the Promised Land, he boldly tells Joshua, "Give me this mountain!" Seeing each day as a mountain to be claimed, you pray, "Give me today!"

God gives everyone a number of days to live. David attests to this in Psalm 139:16—*"Your eyes saw my unformed body. All the days ordained for me were written in your book before one of them came to be."* In Ecclesiastes 3:2, David's son, King Solomon, prescribes everyone with *"a time to be born and a time to die."* Instead of seeing life with a number of days to live, some view life defeated, as though their days are numbered. Your view of your days directly affects the passion and direction of your prayers.

Some pray defensively. They see life as victims enduring life's storms. Others pray offensively. They view life as victors attacking the day. My dad was a victor.

Eaten by cancer and given a short time to live, Dad and I spent a night at the hospital together. The medication for his pain left him delusional. The only way to calm him was to pray together. During one prayer, I saw why God used Dad dramatically for many years. He took both of my hands and earnestly prayed,

"Dear God, we know that you want to do great things. Just show us what you want to do and let us take the lead. Please, God, let us take the lead."

Dad saw each day as a gift and opportunity. Each day was a gift to work with God. Every day was an opportunity to accomplish great things with God. It was Dad's nature to boldly petition God: "God, give me this day to show how great You are."

Do you view each day as a victim or victor? Check your attitude when you wake up each morning. Do you say "Good morning, Lord," or "Good Lord, it's morning"? How you view God affects how you see your days. That's why you begin your prayer with a big picture of God. This is important, for how you view the day is how you live the day. How you perceive the day affects how you pray for the day. That is why Jesus commands us to start the day as victors praying, *"Give us today."*

FOCUS ON YOUR DAY
"our DAILY bread"

Before running out the door each morning shouting "Carpe Diem—Seize the Day," remember, there is more to this prayer than a good attitude. To effectively pray *"Give us today our daily bread,"* you need to see the day correctly before seizing it.

Jesus' adjective "daily" (*epiousios*) carries weight. Scholars formerly believed Matthew's and Luke's accounts of the Lord's Prayer held the only appearance of this word in all Greek literature. Yet decades ago, scholars found it on an ancient papyrus. It was on a woman's shopping list beside items needed that day.[22]

When praying, *"Give us today our daily bread,"* you don't merely ask God to give you the day. You ask Him to provide what you need to win the day. Such prayers are harder than you realize. They require avoiding double vision.

Avoiding Double Vision in Prayer

Spiritual double vision resembles physical double vision. Physical double vision occurs when your two eyes aim at two different targets. As your brain tries to blend the two messages, it blurs your vision. Imagine the difficulty of physically walking, working, or making decisions with double vision. Then imagine the strain of experiencing life that way spiritually. That's why Jesus offers the Lord's Prayer in Matthew 6:9–13, then warns against double vision in verses 19–34.

SEEING TWO TREASURES   In verses 19–21, Jesus explains how one eye looking at treasures on earth and the other staring at treasures of heaven blurs your vision and

---

[22] William Barclay, *The Gospel of Matthew* (Philadelphia: The Westminster Press, 1976).

affects your prayers. To see heavenly treasures alone, focus on what lasts for eternity. Identify it! Then ask God for what you need to secure it.

SEEING WITH TWO EYES: Verses 22–23 speaks of one eye full of light and the other of darkness. Try watching your television when the colors and images from two different programs converge. It is impossible. To clear this up spiritually, align your eyes on what makes you think, live, or act godly. Then, ask God to give you what you need to make what you see a reality.

SEEING TWO MASTERS: Jesus also refers to two masters in verse 24, saying, *"You cannot be slaves of God and of money."* Though many today carry more than one job with more than one boss, Jesus says you cannot have more than one master. You can only answer to one—God. Therefore, check your vision by checking your decisions. Do you say no to God because of something else, or can you say no to everything else because of God? If you see God as your master, He will master your prayers.

SEEING TWO KINGDOMS: Verse 33 implies two kingdoms when Jesus charges you to seek God's kingdom first instead of yours. Your kingdom could be an income bracket, title, or accomplishment. It could seem as well-meaning as having the perfect marriage or family. Yet if you have one eye on your kingdom and another on God's, you will have a blurred vision of both. With both eyes on God's Kingdom, He will give you a clear picture of what you need to ask each day. Amazingly, everything then falls into place.

SEEING TWO TROUBLES: Finally, Jesus identifies two troubles grabbing your attention. In verse 34, He says having one eye on today's troubles with the other eye on tomorrow's blurs your prayers. That's why Jesus recommends you let Him take care of tomorrow so you can focus on praying over the troubles of each day.

The Effects of Double Vision in Prayer

Playing linebacker in high school, a collision with a running back cracked my helmet. It was the strangest experience. Lying face down, I knew the grass was there but couldn't see it. Finally, seeing colors again, I thought it best to get up and walk to the sidelines. The coach appeared to be on the bow of a ship moving up and down. With each step forward, I was taking two to the side. I was the perfect candidate for a breathalyzer test.

The coach met me on the field. Putting his hands to the sides of my helmet he asked, "Becton, are you ok?" I remember saying, "Whoa!" Looking in my eyes and seeing no one home, coach said, "Becton, go sit on the bench."

I was no good to the coach, no good for the team, and was removed from the game all because of blurred vision. The same is true in prayer. You are no good to God, no good to other believers and might as well be sidelined for the day if you begin the day with blurred vision.

Matthew 6:25–34 describes the effects of blurred vision on your prayer life.

²⁵ "This is why I tell you: Don't worry about your life, what you will eat or what you will drink; or about your body, what you will wear. Isn't life more than food and the body more than clothing? ²⁶ Look at the birds of the sky: They don't sow or reap or gather into barns, yet your heavenly Father feeds them. Aren't you worth more than they? ²⁷ Can any of you add a single cubit to his height by worrying? ²⁸ And why do you worry about clothes? Learn how the wildflowers of the field grow: they don't labor or spin thread. ²⁹ Yet I tell you that not even Solomon in all his splendor was adorned like one of these! ³⁰ If that's how God clothes the grass of the field, which is here today and thrown into the furnace tomorrow, won't He do much more for you—you of little faith? ³¹ So don't worry, saying, 'What will we eat?' or 'What will we drink?' or 'What will we wear?' ³² For the idolaters eagerly seek all these things, and your heavenly Father knows that you need them. ³³ But seek first the kingdom of God and His righteousness, and all these things will be provided for you. ³⁴ Therefore don't worry about tomorrow, because tomorrow will worry about itself. Each day has enough trouble of its own."

These verses show how blurred vision adversely affects your prayers.

DOUBLE VISION STRENGTHENS YOUR WORRIES AND WEAKENS YOUR PRAYERS. No wonder the word "worry" appears seven times in these ten verses. Spritual double vision makes it hard to walk, work, and make decisions with God. Furthermore, worry has the same effect spiritually as physically. It weakens you. Drained from worry, you are too tired to pray. That's why you open prayer focusing on God's nature, abilities, Kingdom and will. Tightening your focus lightens your load, weakens your worries, and strengthens your prayers.

DOUBLE VISION INCREASES YOUR REQUESTS AND WASTES YOUR PRAYERS. Double vision may cause you to pray more by seeing twice as much to pray about. You not only see the needs of the day but also tomorrow's. Yet Jesus presses in verses 25–31, "Why pray for what has already been promised?" You pray for food and clothes as if God cares more for the birds and grass than you. David pens in Psalm 37:25, *"I was young and now I am old, yet I have never seen the righteous forsaken or their children begging bread."*

Furthermore, you pray for more time as if doing so adds hours to your days or days to your life. Yet Job 14:5 states, *"Man's days are determined; you have decreed the number of his months and have set limits he cannot exceed."* Therefore, do not pray for things beyond your control or what God has already promised. You are wasting precious time with God in prayer. God is in charge of tomorrow. You are responsible for today. God wants you to see the needs of the day, then pray for those needs and seize the day.

Achieving Nearsightedness in Prayer

Praying *"Give us today our daily bread"* requires spiritual myopia—nearsightedness. Over one third of the population suffers physically from nearsightedness. This visual handicap only sees items up close while distant objects blur.[23]

Spiritual myopia is helpful when praying for daily bread. It means having to...

1. Keep that which is close to God close to you.
2. Make that which is clear to God clear to you.
3. Let that which is not of God be a blur to you.
4. Pray for today and trust God for tomorrow.

Abraham Lincoln said, "The best thing about the future is that it comes only one day at a time." Therefore, focus on the day. See it and seize it. You will be addressing your needs of the future when you ask for the bread of each day.

ASK FOR YOUR BREAD
"our daily BREAD"

"Bread" is often used metaphorically in the New Testament.[24] In Jesus' model prayer, "bread" refers to our

---

[23] Hiroko O'Leary, Japan. Today's Christian Woman, "Small Talk."

[24] The word "bread" appears 297 times in the Old Testament and 99 times in the New Testament. New Testament references are more metaphorical than Old Testament. In John 6:48, Jesus announces, *"I am the bread of life."* In Luke 22:19, Jesus breaks the bread of communion saying, *"This is My body, which is given for you. Do this in remembrance of me."*

needs, not wants. It's not that God is disinterested in our wants. Psalm 37:4 reads, *"Delight yourself in the LORD and he will give you the desires of your heart."* Look at the progression of the Lord's Prayer. The right perspective of God leads to right priorities, and right priorities focus on necessities, not luxuries. Still, how do you distinguish necessities from luxuries? According to Solomon, it sometimes takes limiting yourself to praying a single sentence.

On the eve of Solomon's coronation, God offers, *"Ask. What should I give you?"* (1 Kings 3:5) He could ask for anything. Yet before asking, Solomon reflects on God's kindness to his dad, King David (v.6). Then he considers God's purpose for his life...to rule over Israel (v.7–8). With the weight of God's righteousness over him and the burden of God's responsibility upon him, Solomon can't think of luxuries. He needs God's help to fulfill God's plan. Thus, he sums up his request in one sentence. Solomon prays, *"So give your servant an obedient heart to judge your people and to discern between good and evil."* (v. 9)

In order to pray for necessities, not luxuries, learn from Solomon. Before asking God for anything,

- *Reflect on the person of God.* His character alone will shape your prayer.
- *Consider the purpose of God.* Striving to fulfill His Kingdom and will each day focuses your prayer.
- *Limit your prayer to God.* If God gave you one sentence, what would you ask? This

exercise peels away the luxuries and leaves only the necessities for the day. What remains is your bread.

This simple exercise supplies you with daily bread. Now with bread in hand, live each day confidently and competently for God.

HOLDING YOUR BREAD
"Attacking Each Day"

Apparently, holding a piece of bread changes your view of life. I once read of an orphanage in Europe after World War II. As caregivers put the children to bed, they cried themselves to sleep. Those in charge used night-lights, played soft music, and repeatedly told the children everything was fine. Yet nothing consoled them. The crying stopped one night when they tried something strange. Each child received a slice of bread to hold in bed.

Someone on staff realized many of these children survived on the streets. Their diet was whatever they found or stole. They lived without any guarantee of food that day or the next. Their slice of bread in bed became their guarantee. No matter what they faced the next day, they knew they would survive.

God wants you to know, regardless what you face each day, you will survive. No matter what He asks you to do or endure each day, you have what you need to fulfill it. You can live each day confidently, if you start the day with your daily bread (2 Corinthians 9:8). Holding your bread in hand, you can eagerly end your prayer saying,

> *"Since you have given me all I need today*
> *to accomplish all you want today,*
> *then Lord, I have one last request.*
> *Give me this day!"*

Chapter 6

PRAYING FOR FORGIVENESS

John Stott tells of a leading British humanist interviewed on television. She vulnerably divulges,

> What I envy most about you Christians
> is your forgiveness.
> I have nobody to forgive me.[25]

She unknowingly speaks for Christians and non-Christians alike. All want to be forgiven and able to forgive, for doing so provides great benefits. Researchers at Hope College in Michigan report that one's blood pressure, heart rate, and muscle tension all increase as forgiveness decreases.[26] Furthermore, two Stanford studies underscore the obvious.

---

[25] John Stott, "Freedom," <u>Preaching Today</u>, Tape No. 102.
[26] Eileen O'Connor, "Forgiveness Heals the Heart, Research Hints" (<u>http://www.cnn.com/HEALTH/9905/20/forgiveness/</u>), May 20, 1999.

Forgivers hurt less and have better interpersonal relationships. Essentially, life is better when you learn to forgive.[27]

Regretfully, many turn to secular research for step-by-step programs of forgiveness when God patented it in scripture long ago. In the Lord's Prayer, Jesus teaches us to pray,

*"And forgive us our debts
as we also have forgiven our debtors."*
– Matthew 6:12

This single verse acts as a master key. It not only unlocks other biblical truths about forgiveness, but also spotlights four stages of forgiveness.

ACKNOWLEDGING YOUR NEED FOR FORGIVENESS

The first stage of forgiveness requires acknowledging your need for forgiveness. Jesus stresses this in Matthew 6:12. According to His model prayer, Jesus says you need forgiveness if you hope to fulfill your day and debt.

The Need to Fulfill Your Day

The ripple effect of forgiveness actually begins in Matthew 6:11. There Jesus teaches us to pray, *"Give us today our daily bread."* We ask God to fill our needs for the day in order

---

[27] Carl E. Thoresen, "Stanford Forgiveness Project" (Stanford Center for Research in Disease Prevention, Stanford University; http://www. stanford.edu/~alexsox/forgiveness_article.htm).

to win the day. Every word is important in scripture. The simple word "and" is an important rock in the pond of the Lord's Prayer. Its ripple connects verses 12 and 13 to verse 11, making it a single petition. Look at verses 11–13,

> [11] *"Give us today our daily bread.*
> [12] *And forgive us our debts,*
>   *as we also have forgiven our debtors.*
> [13] *And do not bring us into temptation,*
>   *but deliver us from the evil one."*

Reading verses 11–13 as one request highlights an uncomfortable truth. Like manna in the Old Testament, God's bread lasts a day. Sadly, we burn it off before noon carrying the unnecessary weight of unforgivness. Yet, our walk becomes stronger and steps lighter by releasing what needs to be forgiven. The act of releasing means learning how to forgive and be forgiven.

The Need to Fulfill Your Debt

Jesus describes the burden of forgiveness as "debt" in verse 12. It's one of five Greek words used in the New Testament to describe sin. They include...

"Harmartia"
Literally means "to miss the mark."
It is the sin of compromise—settling for less.
God set the bar and you didn't reach it.

"Paraptoma"
Literally means "to slide across."
It is the unintentional sin—when ungodly
emotions take you too far.
God drew the line, and you slid across it.

"Parabasis"
Literally means "to step across."
It is the intentional sin—knowing it is wrong
but doing it anyway.
God drew the line, you stepped across it.
(*This is the word used in Luke's account of
the Lord's Prayer*)

"Anomia"
Literally means "lawlessness."
It is the sin of contempt—disregarding everything of God.
You do what you want with no fear of God.

"Opheilema"
Literally means "debt."
It is the obligation of sin—you owe God.
You missed, slid, stepped, or just didn't care,
but now, you owe God!

Matthew's account of the Lord's Prayer appropriately uses "debt." "Debt" underscores our accountability. Regardless of why or how we sinned, we owe God (Romans 6:23). It also magnifies our need for God's forgiveness.

At the Washington Monument, a little boy tells a guard, "I want to buy it." Stooping, the guard asks, "How much do you have?" Showing the guard his quarter, the guard quips, "Boy, that's not enough." Pulling out nine cents more, the lad adds, "I thought you'd say that." His eyes squinting a smile, the guard explains, "Son, you need to understand three things. First, thirty-four cents is not enough. In fact, $34 million is not enough to buy the Washington Monument. Second, the Washington Monument is not for sale. And third, if you are an American citizen, it already belongs to you."[28]

Similarly, you can offer God good deeds for your debt, but no amount of good deeds will buy God's forgiveness. Besides, it's not for sale. It has already been purchased for you by Jesus' blood. Therefore, if you want God's forgiveness, you just need to ask.

ASKING GOD FOR FORGIVENESS

The second stage of God's forgiveness involves asking Him. However, simply asking God's forgiveness involves more than it sounds.

A Specific Agreement

God's forgiveness requires a specific agreement. 1 John 1:9 explains:

> [9] *If we confess our sins, He is faithful and right-*
> *eous to forgive us our sins and to cleanse us from*
> *all unrighteousness.*

---

[28] James S. Hewett, *Illustrations Unlimited* (Wheaton: Tyndale House Publishers, Inc, 1988) pp. 218–219.

The Greek word for "confess" means "to say the same" … "to agree with God." When asking His forgiveness, God wants us to agree with Him specifically and repentantly about our sins. Yet, our confessions are often general instead of specific. We pray, "God, forgive me of all my sins, those I know about and don't know about." Sweat would pour, however, if God audibly replied, "What sins? I'll not forgive them unless you name them."

Sadly, we give more attention to our financial debt than our spiritual debt. We know every penny owed to every creditor. But, when it comes to our sins, we hide them in generalities. God wants us responsible for our sins. We do so by specifically naming them.

Furthermore, we agree with God not only when calling them by name but also by walking away from them. That's repentance. Acts 26:20 says you prove your repentance by your deeds. Asking God's forgiveness for a specific sin and still doing it sends a conflicting message. With your words you say, "God, I am sorry," yet your actions tell Him, "I'm not stopping." That doesn't clear the debt of sin; it only increases it.

When confessing sins God's way (agreeing and turning), we experience something supernatural—God canceling our debt.

A Canceled Debt

One of God's endearing attributes is His desire and ability to erase your debt. Psalm 103:12 says upon confession He removes your sins as far as the east is from the west. If you are always facing east, you never see west. When you ask God's forgiveness, He puts your sins behind Him, never seeing them again. Furthermore, in Jeremiah 31:34, God promises to remember your sins no more. That's usually our problem with forgiveness. We forget our sin and guilt for a while, but occasionally, fish them out again. Corrie ten Boom alludes to this in her book, *Tramp for the Lord*:

> It was 1947…I had come from Holland to defeated Germany with the message that God forgives. It was the truth they needed most to hear in that bitter, bombed-out land, and I gave them my favorite mental picture. Maybe because the sea is never far from a Hollander's mind, I like to think that that's where forgiven sins are thrown. "When we confess our sins," I said, "God casts them into the deepest ocean, gone forever… Then God places a sign out there that says No Fishing Allowed!"[29]

God doesn't fish for forgiven sins, and you shouldn't fish for the guilt from them. If confessed the way God asked, He forgave and forgot them the way He promised. When asking God's forgiveness, trust He cancels the debt. Live forgiven!

ACCEPTING RESPONSIBILITY TO FORGIVE

We now move to the third stage of forgiveness… forgiving others. It may be the most challenging. C. S. Lewis

---

[29] Ibid., 217.

---

confesses, "We all agree that forgiveness is a beautiful idea until we have to practice it."[30] An older pastor confronted Loree and me with this.

Doing ministry is hard enough without the extra baggage of unforgiveness. Over thirty years of settling squabbles between members, watching believers fight for traditions instead of the great commission, and being punched with direct and indirect criticism left its toll. Loree and I asked to meet with an older pastor to counsel us. Being a pastor, he sympathetically listened to our history. Then our caring older brother said, "Your view of everthying is skewed by cateracts of unforgiveness."

Gently he explained, "Unforgiveness clouds your eyes and distorts your view of God, yourself, others, and God's activity around you. Remove those cateracts and life will be clearer, even ligther."

We can carry wounds so long we not only doubt their healing, we can't picture life without them. That's why many question their capacity to forgive and even avoid (intentionally or unintentionally) the effort to forgive. Unknowingly, many of us pay a daily price for our oversized luggage of unforgiveness. So, let's open it up.

The Capacity to Forgive

Our older mentor reminded us that it's Jesus' nature to forgive. At salvation, Jesus' Spirit enters us giving us the

---

[30] Edythe Draper, *Draper's Book of Quotations for the Christian World* (Wheaton: Tyndale House Publishers, Inc., 1992). Entries 4103–4106.

opportunity to tap into His nature. Romans 5:8 reminds us Jesus loves us at our worst. 1 John 1:9 says He offers forgiveness at our peak of sinfulness. That's His nature. And with His nature in us, we have the capcity to forgive...and are fulfilled when we do.

Furthermore, our capactity to forgive comes from experience. Jesus' parable in Matthew 18:21–35 highlights this. He tells of a slave owing his master 10,000 talents. It's a ridiculous amount that would have taken him 160,000 years to pay back.[31] After the master forgives this insurmountable debt, the slave finds someone who owes him 100 denarii, a day's wage.[32] He chokes him, demanding immediate payment.

It was uncomfortable when my older brother had me read this parable and connect the dots. Jesus forgave me of an impossible debt. There was no way I could pay the debt for my sin. Jesus did that for me.

Then, my friend pointed to my bulging baggage of unforgiveness. Opening it up and pulling out what others had said—harsh statements I rehearsed again and again—he said, "How severe is this compared to all Jesus forgave you?" He held up my disappointments in others. Grudges I held for those who didn't help me, stand up for me, or come to my aid like I did them. Again he pressed, "How painful would it be for you to forgive them compared to all Jesus went through to forgive you?"

---

[31] http://text.watv.org/english/qna/view.html?idx=1573
[32] Ibid.

He made his point. Actually, Jesus made the point long ago. As Jesus' followers, we have His nature within us. We have His capacity to forgive. And when we think someone's offence is too much to forgive, stop and compare it to all Jesus went through to forgive you and me. Suddenly, our effort to forgive doesn't seem so demanding.

Choosing to Forgive

Though Jesus' nature within us gives us the capacity to forgive, our human nature makes it hard. That's why we have to work at forgiveness. Our older brother explained to Loree and me how using an imaginary chair helps him. Though it sounds childish, it's a good tool. He taught,

> Imagine a chair before you and the one you need to forgive sitting in it. Now, be specific. Tell them what they did to offend and wound you. Don't stop there. Explain how you feel about what they did or didn't do. But before letting them out of the chair, tell them out loud, "I forgive you. You owe me nothing." Keep repeating it until you know you mean it and feel released from the weight of any unforgiveness you carry toward them.

Knowing the nature of some who wounded us, Loree and I asked our friend, "But what if they continue hurting us?" Smiling from experience, he said, "Put them back in the chair.

I've had to do it a lot with some in my life." Then he added, "Besides, it's what Jesus taught and modeled."

Pastor to pastor, he took me back to Matthew 18:21–24. Here's what prompted Jesus to tell the story of the unforgiving slave:

> [21] *Then Peter came to Him and said, "Lord, how many times could my brother sin against me and I forgive him? As many as seven times?"*
> [22] *"I tell you, not as many as seven," Jesus said to him, "but 70 times seven.* [23] *For this reason, the kingdom of heaven can be compared to a king who wanted to settle accounts with his slaves."*

Jesus knew we would have to forgive some repeatedly. That's why He put *"70 times seven"* in scripture. For the accoutants, that does not mean you can stop forgiving them after 490 times in the chair. It means you keep on forgiving them the way Jesus forgives you—repeatedly.

When I need someone other than Jesus to inspire me to forgive, I think of Clara Barton. She founded the American Red Cross. Being reminded of a vicious deed done to her years ago, she acted as if she never heard of it. "Don't you remember it?" her friend asked. "No," Barton replied, "I distinctly remember forgetting it."[33]

---

[33] Luis Palau, "Experiencing God's Forgiveness," <u>Christianity Today</u>, Vol. 34, no. 1.

Because we usually default to our human nature instead of Jesus' nature within us, we have to work at forgiving. It must be a choice. But when we choose to forgive, we experience intimacy with Jesus, and the fulfillment of forgiving like Him.

ENJOYING THE FREEDOM OF FORGIVENESS

In case I have not made it clear, everything about forgiveness is hard. Asking God's forgiveness requires agreeing with God regarding our sin. Our pride fights us each time we try. More challenging than that, however, is giving forgiveness to others. Entitlement guards our grudges. It tells us, "You have every right not to forgive them." That's when Corrie ten Boom reminds you, "You're hurting yourself when you fail to forgive." Though her story has become popular, it's worth repeating.

Under Nazi Germany's brutal hand, Ms. Boom's family hid refuges from 1942–44. She and her family were arrested in 1944 and sent to notorious Ravensbrück in Germany. There they endured indescribable indignities leading to the death of her sister Betsie.[34]

Years after being libertated from the camp, Ms. Boom came face to face with one of the guards. The cruelest of all guards now stood before her. Extending his hand, he

---

[34] Sam Wellman, "Heroes of History" (http://www.heroesofhistory.com/page59.html).

asks, "Will you forgive me?" In her writings, Ms. Boom vividly explains:

> "I stood there with coldness clutching at my heart, but I know that the will can function regardless of the temperature of the heart. I prayed, Jesus, help me! Woodenly, mechanically I thrust my hand into the one stretched out to me and I experienced an incredible thing. The current started in my shoulder, raced down into my arms and sprang into our clutched hands. Then this warm reconciliation seemed to flood my whole being, bringing tears to my eyes. 'I forgive you, brother,' I cried with my whole heart. For a long moment we grasped each other's hands, the former guard, the former prisoner. I have never known the love of God so intensely as I did in that moment! To forgive is to set a prisoner free and discover the prisoner was you."[35]

"To forgive is to set the prisoner free and discover the prisoner was you." What a powerful statement. What a dynamic experience. What an earnest desire for anyone needing freedom from unforgiveness.

---

[35] James S. Hewett, *Illustrations Unlimited* (Wheaton: Tyndale House Publishers, Inc, 1988) p. 218.

Use the questions below to assess where you are with forgiveness needed from God, or forgiveness you need to give others.

Regarding Forgiveness from God...

- Are you still imprisoned by unconfessed and unforgiven sins?
- Do you live in a cell of silence, unable to freely walk and talk with God?
- When you do talk, are there certain subjects you avoid?
- Wouldn't you like to confess those sins, receive God's forgiveness and experience freedom with God?

Regarding Forgiving Others...

- Are you imprisoned by your unwillingness to forgive someone who wronged you?
- Are you looking at life through the bars of your own anger and bitterness?
- Isn't it time to forgive them, experience God's love, and be free?
- Corrie ten Boom says, "To forgive is to set the prisoner free and discover the prisoner was you."

In order to live free again, Jesus reminds us to constantly pray,

> *"Forgive us our debts, as we have forgiven our debtors."*[36]

---

[36] There's one more motivator of forgiveness found in verse 12. It's the tiny Greek word "hoos." It's translated "as we have" and means "in proportion to." Understanding this and connecting Matthew 6:12 to verse 14–15, we hear God forgives us in the same amount and manner that we forgive others. What a sobering thought when we feel justified to withhold forgiveness from others.

Chapter 7

PRAYING
WHEN TEMPTED

Hall of Fame catcher Yogi Berra sat behind home plate with the score tied. With two outs in the bottom of the ninth inning, the batter made the sign of the cross on home plate with his bat. Berra, also a Catholic, wiped off the plate and told the batter, "Why don't we let God just watch this game?"[37]

Some are content to let God just watch their lives; others know they will never win without God's involvement. A survey conducted by *Discipleship Journal* proves it. Their readers rank the following as their top spiritual challenges:

1. Materialism   5. (Tie) Anger/Bitterness
2. Pride   5. (Tie) Sexual lust
3. Self-centeredness   7. Envy
4. Laziness   8. Gluttony
     9. Lying

---

[37] James S. Hewett, *Illustrations Unlimited* (Wheaton: Tyndale House Publishers, Inc, 1988), p. 424.

Furthermore, 81% of the readers say these temptations increase when they neglect their time with God, and 84% say they can resist them when involving God through prayer.[38]

This survey confirms Jesus' teaching on prayer. You cannot live fulfilled without asking God to get involved. Matthew 6:11–13 cries for God's involvement.

> [11] *"Give us today our daily bread.*
> [12] *And forgive us our debts,*
> *as we also have forgiven our debtors.*
> [13] *And do not brings us into temptation,*
> *but deliver us from the evil one."*

The word "and" opens verses 12 and 13 connecting them both to verse 11. They link an important sequence in prayer. For God to help you win the day, you need to fulfill your debts to Him and others. Then to remain debt free, ask God to lead you from temptation and deliver you from evil. Verse 13 emphasizes you will not win at life without God's leading and protection. That is why we need a sobering view of our susceptibility to temptation.

UNDERSTANDING TEMPTATION

Regarding temptation remember, God allows it to build us, not break us. And through the temptation, God reveals to us and others where He stands in our lives. It's hard to see this

---

[38] Discipleship Journal, 11–12/92. "To Verify," Leadership.

when battling temptation. That may be why Jesus includes it in His model prayer. He knows we need to understand it and pray over it regularly.

Temptation is a test that can build or break you.
Peirasmos (pi-ras-mos') is the Greek word translated "temptation" in verse 13. It refers to a "test" or "trial." According to James 1, temptation can build or break you. Verses 2–4 emphasize how trials build you.

> *2 Consider it a great joy, my brothers, whenever you experience various trials, 3 knowing that the testing of your faith produces endurance. 4 But endurance must do its complete work, so that you may be mature and complete, lacking nothing.*

The word "trials" in verse 2 appears in the Lord's Prayer as "temptation." According to James' account, we welcome temptations for they spiritually mature us. Yet a difference surfaces between welcoming trials in verse 2 and warning against temptation in verses 13–14:

> *13 No one undergoing a trial should say, "I am being tempted by God." For God is not tempted by evil, and He Himself doesn't tempt anyone. 14 But each person is tempted when he is drawn away and enticed by his own evil desires.*

The words "tempted" and "tempting" in verses 13–14 are the same Greek word translated as "trial" in verse 2. Though "tested" or "tempted" uses the same Greek word, here's the difference. God tests to build you and Satan tempts to break you. According to scripture,

> Satan tempts you to maul you.
> *He is the prowling lion (1 Peter 5:8).*
> God tests you to mature you.
> *He is the loving parent (James 1:4).*
>
> Satan tempts you to bring you down.
> *As a liar, he wants to ruin you (James 1:14–15).*
> God tests you to give you a crown.
> *As the Lord, He wants to reward you (James 1:12).*

God administers tests and allows temptation.

It surprises many that God administers tests and allows temptations. In Genesis 22:1–18, God tests Abraham asking him to sacrifice his only son, Isaac. God promised Abraham a linage as numerous as the sands of the earth (Gen. 12:1–2; 15:1–4). But with Sarah in her eighties and Abraham his nineties, they had not seen their first grain of sand. Taking matters in their own hands, Abraham had a son through Sarah's servant, Hagar. This was not God's will (Gen. 15:1–4)
.

After Isaac was born, God tests Abraham to see if he trusted Him or would once again take matters in his own hands. When

God asks Abraham to sacrifice Isaac, Abraham could have said, "No, God! You promised me a lineage. I won't let you do this." Instead, Abraham trusts God to keep His promise either by raising Isaac to life or providing another son. He trusts and obeys God completely. Of course, God didn't let Abraham sacrifice Isaac. God just wanted Abraham to pass the test.

In my Ph.D. studies, I learned about administering tests. I thought taking tests was hard until having to write one. A good test measures the student's comprehension and mastery of the information. If the test is too easy or hard you will not get a true measurement. The test has to be balanced and fair.

God's tests are always balanced and fair. They show how much you know His will and ways. This involves more than reciting information. God's tests deal with life application. How well do you apply what you know to life's circumstances? Remember, a lot of God's tests are pop quizzes. It is not something you cram for overnight. However, the mornings and nights you spend with God in prayer and His Word prepare you for each day's tests.

Many are also conflicted by the thought that God allows temptation. You see this in Matthew 4:1 where it reads, *"Then Jesus was led by the Spirit into the desert to be tempted by the devil."* There's the word "peirasmos" again. When in Satan's hand, it means tempting you to break you. In God's hand, it means testing you to build you. Yet in this case, God allows temptation as a test, for temptation is the kind of test God cannot administer.

Remember, James 1:13 states, *"When tempted, no one should say, 'God is tempting me.' For God cannot be tempted by evil, nor does he tempt anyone."* God is not evil, nor does He administer anything evil. By living in a world where evil abounds, however, you have to be strong when facing it. Satan administers temptation to make you stumble from God. God allows those temptations to strengthen your submission to Him. James 4:7 states, *"Therefore, submit to God. But resist the devil, and he will flee from you."* God allows Satan to tempt you in order to strengthen your ability to say "No" to him.

WHY GOD ADMINISTERS TESTS AND ALLOWS TEMPTATION

Union-Pacific Railroad constructed an elaborate trestle bridge over a canyon. Before passengers rode across, the construction engineer tested the bridge's strength. Weighting a train down two times its normal payload, he drove it onto the bridge where it remained for the day. When a co-worker complained, "Are you trying to break this bridge?" the engineer answered, "No, I'm trying to prove the bridge is unbreakable."[39]

At times the weight of tests and temptation feels unbearable. Remember God, the engineer, made you. He knows what you can withstand. Furthermore, He wants to prove you are unbreakable, not to Himself, but to you and others.

To show you where you are

---

[39] Michael P. Green, ed., *1500 Illustrations for Biblical Preaching* (Grand Rapids, Michigan: Baker Books, 2001), 373.

When God tests Abraham, He knows the strength of Abraham's faith. But, Abraham didn't. Imagine Abraham's confidence walking away from the altar with Isaac under his arm. Discovering he is willing to submit everything to God makes Abraham more open to do anything with God.

There are times God tests you to show you can withstand more than you realize and accomplish more than you think.

To show others what can be done

God tests Abraham not only to prove something to Abraham, but also to Isaac. Isaac sees his dad's true character. He learns his dad lives what he taught. Isaac realizes in their family everything, including him, belongs to God.

Sometimes God tests you knowing someone else is watching. God wants them to see the true character of your surrender. He wants your walk to illustrate your talk. He wants them to see the strength of a life when everything belongs to God. And remember, that someone watching may be your daughter or son.

To show Satan where he stands

Finally, God allows Satan to tempt you so you can show Satan where he stands. That's the reason God allows Satan to attack Job in Job 1:8–12.

> [8] *Then the Lord said to Satan, "Have you considered My servant Job? No one else on earth is like him, a man of perfect integrity, who fears*

God and turns away from evil."
⁹ Satan answered the Lord, "Does Job fear God for nothing? ¹⁰ Haven't You placed a hedge around him, his household, and everything he owns? You have blessed the work of his hands, and his possessions have increased in the land. ¹¹ But stretch out Your hand and strike everything he owns, and he will surely curse You to Your face." ¹² "Very well," the Lord told Satan, "everything he owns is in your power. However, you must not lay a hand on Job himself." So Satan left the Lord's presence.

Satan attacks Job financially. He loses everything he owns. Satan attacks Job emotionally. With his children dead, he loses everything he loves. Satan attacks Job physically covering him with sores, and socially when his wife and friends turn on him. Yet Job 1:22 records, *"In all this, Job did not sin by charging God with wrongdoing."* Job shows Satan his love for and life with God are unbreakable.

HOW TO PRAY REGARDING TEMPTATION

Since tests and temptation are a part of life, what do you do to make sure they build you instead of break you? Jesus says pray about it. In Matthew 6:13, Jesus prays, *"And, lead us not into temptation."* In fact, there are four specific prayers regarding tests and temptation.

"God, don't allow too much."

Praying, "God, please don't allow too much," assures you by reminding you God only allows temptations you are strong enough to resist. 1 Corinthians 10:13 promises,

> *[13] No temptation has overtaken you except what is common to humanity. God is faithful, and He will not allow you to be tempted beyond what you are able, but with the temptation He will also provide a way of escape so that you are able to bear it.*

Listen to it again. God promises not to *"allow you to be tempted beyond what you are able."* It seems silly to pray for something God already promised. But when praying, "God, please don't allow too much temptation," it reminds you He never does. Therefore, you know you have the strength to resist any temptation you face.

"God, wake me before I fall."

Praying, "God, wake me before I fall," comes from Jesus' charge to Peter, James, and John in Matthew 26:40–41. The three are with Jesus in Gethsemane the night before He's crucified. Jesus struggles praying while they struggled to stay awake.

> *[40] Then He came to the disciples and found them sleeping. He asked Peter, "So, couldn't you stay awake with Me one hour? [41] Stay awake and pray,*

*so that you won't enter into temptation. The spirit
is willing, but the flesh is weak."*

Jesus commands them to "watch and pray." The word
"watch" means to be "awake" or "alert" and is a one-time
order. "Pray," on the other hand, sounds Jesus' continual
charge. Combining the two, Jesus says, "Wake up and keep
praying. You are about to fall into temptation."

Ask Jesus to do for you as He did His disciples. Anytime
He sees you unconscious to an oncoming temptation, ask Him
to wake you and call you to prayer. Regarding temptation,
Mark Twain was right: "It is easier to stay out than to get out."
Therefore, pray and ask God to wake you up and call you to
prayer before you fall.

"God, show me your way out when I go too far."

If you find yourself succumbing to temptation, trust 1
Corinthians 13 and pray, "God, show me your way out when I
go too far." There God promises, *"But when you are tempted,
he will also provide a way out so that you can stand up under
it."* Like exit signs in buildings, God clearly marks His way
out. You just need to know what to look for in advance.

Spending the night in a hotel, Loree and I were awakened
by the fire alarm. A voice through the speaker system says,
"There is a fire in the hotel. Please make your way to the
nearest exit." Finding the map posted in our room, Loree
traces the exit route with her finger. Because of my poor sense
of direction, if finding the way out was left to me, we'd die.

As we head toward the exit, several pass by going the opposite direction. Obviously, these were other directionally challenged husbands. Loree calls out, "Where are you going? The nearest exit is this way." The strangest thing happens. Everyone stops to hear Loree. Some turn and follow, but others continue the wrong way. Fortunately, there was no fire and no one was hurt; but, consider the consequences had the fire been real.

All of Satan's temptations are real, as are the consequences. Therefore, when temptation comes, God sounds the alarm to awaken you. He counts on you to recognize His exit signs. One of the most evident signs is the voice in your head saying, "This is wrong." That's your first clue to exit the situation. Other exit signs may be Bible verses or spiritual songs coming to mind. You might imagine the consequences if you continue. A phone may ring, door open, or friends cross your path just at the right time. God can present all of these as your way out from temptation. However, like those in the hallway, once the exit is shown, it is up to you to take it.

"God, give me what I need to pass the test."

You may think you walked away from God's exit so many times you will never escape. Then, you bitterly muse, "God is perfect, He has never experienced the power of temptation and doesn't understand what I'm going through. He does not know what is truly needed to pass the test."

These thoughts are understandable, but inaccurate. John 1:14 reminds us that God *"became flesh and made his dwelling among us."* Putting on flesh and living among us as Jesus, God experienced every temptation we face, and passed each test. Hebrews 2:18 asserts, *"Because he himself suffered when he was tempted, he is able to help those who are being tempted."*

In the summer of 1989, Mark Wellman, a paraplegic, received national recognition climbing the sheer granite face of El Capitan in Yosemite National Park. How did he do it? He had help. Wellman rode the shoulders of his climbing companion, Mike Corbett, who climbed it three times before.[40]

No matter how tall your mountain of temptation, Jesus has already conquered it. Trust the strength of His shoulders. He promises to help you conquer any temptation you face.

THE LABELS OF TEMPTATION

Depending on the outcome of your struggle with temptation, you receive one of two labels. If the temptation repeatedly conquers you, you are labeled "addicted." Yet if you repeatedly conquer your tests and temptation, God labels you "approved."

As explained earlier, James 1 uses the Greek word *peirasmos* to refer to tests administered by God and temptations from Satan. In verse 3, however, a different Greek word appears for "testing." It says, *"you know that the testing of your faith*

---

[40] Greg Asimakoupoulos in *Fresh Illustrations for Preaching & Teaching* (Baker), from the editors of Leadership.

develops perseverance." The Greek word here is *dokimion* (dok-im'-ee-on). Ron Lee Davis explains its significance:

> That's the Greek term dokimas, and it literally means "someone or something that has been put to the test and has measured up." If you have ever traveled to the Middle East, you may have taken note of the fact that you can visit a potter and you will look at a vessel, a jar, and it's been through the furnace, and it's been through the fire, and it hasn't cracked. It hasn't broken; it comes out whole. It comes out complete. And you turn that jar over, and on the bottom there is stamped DOKIAMAS. It means "approved." This is a vessel of character. It has withstood the test of the furnace where it has been refined, and it hasn't broken; it is whole, complete. That's character.[41]

What a gift when God labels you "approved!" That means He knows you withstood the fires of tests and temptation. He can count on you. It also means when Satan looks at you he sees "approved!" He's tried again and again to break you, but the fires of the challenge only strengthened you. You are unbreakable. Finally, it means when others look at you they see "approved!" They see it in the consistent display of your

---

[41] Ron Lee Davis, "Rejoicing in Our Suffering," *Preaching Today*, Tape 74.

character. You are authentic.

If God labels you, where would He place it? The pottery owners placed it underneath the jars. In my opinion, the most appropriate place God could write "approved!" is on your knees. Only through prayer will you be able to pass the tests and come through the fires of temptation "approved!"

Chapter 8

PRAYING FOR DELIVERANCE

The only safe war is when you are nine years old and the battle is with neighborhood friends. Under the blue skies of a Saturday afternoon, the energized voices of five boys echoed from a backyard. We had just captured someone from the opposing force. Poor Robby was our lone POW. We tied him to a tree behind a work shed, and told him to tell us were his troops were. If Robby had a rank and serial number, that's all he would have given. Since he didn't have those, he stood against the tree, tied up and tight-lipped.

Getting nowhere with Robby, we decided to look for others. As each of us darted away, Robby pleaded, "Guys, don't leave me here." With each of us secure behind a bush, tree or car, Robby screamed, "Guys, come back! Don't leave me tied up!" We rushed back to hear Robby say, "Come on, guys, untie me. Let me loose. I can't stand it anymore."

Robby's words come to mind when I consider others feeling tied up and left alone. You feel...

tied by an addiction	pressed by depression
bound by bitterness	held back by hopelessness
wrapped with fear	gripped by guilt
	... __(add your own)__

You feel bound and abandoned. You can't stand it any more. You want to be free. You want deliverance. In Matthew 6:13, Jesus says if you want deliverance, ask God. Specifically pray, *"And do not bring us into temptation, but deliver us from the evil one."* Jesus says, "Ask God to deliver you."

Being unbound, however, does not liberate you to live unbridled. Warren Wiersbe writes this wise disclaimer:

> Freedom does not mean I am able to do whatever I want to do. That's the worst kind of bondage. Freedom means I have been set free to become all that God wants me to be, to achieve all that God wants me to achieve, to enjoy all that God wants me to enjoy.[42]

If bound by something and you want God to deliver you, look closely at God's conditions of deliverance in Matthew 6:13.

---

[42] Edythe Draper, *Draper's Book of Quotations for the Christian World* (Wheaton: Tyndale House Publishers, Inc., 1992). Entries 4122–4124.

...FROM "THE EVIL"

In verse 13, Jesus instructs us to pray, *"And do not bring us into temptation, but deliver us from the evil one."* The word "one" is not in the original text. It reads, "...deliver us from the evil." However, since the article "the" appears before the word "evil," it classifies it as the ultimate evil, the evil of Satan. That's why some translators take liberties writing "the evil one" instead of leaving it as "the evil."

Personally, I like it as originally written. Asking for deliverance from "the evil" not only identifies the individual behind the evil, it also includes his intent and the instruments he uses.

Satan's Intent

Jesus explains in John 12:39–40 Satan's evil intent is to blind, bind, and destroy:

> *39 This is why they were unable to believe, because Isaiah also said:*
> *40 "He has blinded their eyes*
> *and hardened their hearts,*
> *so that they would not see with their eyes*
> *or understand with their hearts,*
> *and be converted,*
> *and I would heal them."*

Satan aims to blind unbelievers of who Jesus is and all He offers. He wants to blind them to bind and keep them from turning to Jesus for salvation. If saved, Satan desires to blind you to who you are and all you have in Jesus. This keeps you from experiencing and accomplishing God's plans for you.

The longer Satan blinds and binds you, the closer he comes to his ultimate intent...destroying you. James 1:13–15 warns,

> *13 No one undergoing a trial should say, "I am being tempted by God." For God is not tempted by evil, and He Himself doesn't tempt anyone. 14 But each person is tempted when he is drawn away and enticed by his own evil desires. 15 Then after desire has conceived, it gives birth to sin, and when sin is fully grown, it gives birth to death.*

Satan's evil never discriminates. If unsaved, Satan wants to blind and bind you long enough to destroy any hope of your salvation with God. If saved, Satan schemes to blind and bind you long enough to destroy your service to God.

Satan's Instrument

Though Satan's intent is clear, the instruments he uses are not. Jesus explains in John 8:44 Satan's chief instrument is deception.

> *44 "You are of your father the Devil, and you want to carry out your father's desires. He was a murderer from the beginning and has not stood in the truth, because there is no truth in him. When*

*he tells a lie, he speaks from his own nature,
because he is a liar and the father of liars."*

Satan uses a subtle combination of lies to blind and bind you. The first lie may seem small and insignificant, yet when combined with others, it shuts you down. Something similar happened in 1995.

A squirrel climbs on the Metro-North Railroad power lines near New York City setting off an electrical surge. The surge weakens an overhead bracket causing a wire to dangle toward the tracks. The wire catches a passing train, tearing down all lines, and tying up 47,000 commuters for hours. It all starts with a squirrel on a power line.[43]

What was your squirrel on the line? What was the first harmless lie Satan gave you? Was it...

- The Bible just contains God's Word – it's not the Word of God.
- Jesus is one way to God – He is not the only way to God.
- There are no absolutes – except that there are no absolutes.
- Recklessly drink, watch, hear and say what you want. It won't affect you.
- You have already sinned this much, you might as well go all the way.

---

[43] Sherman L. Burford, Fairmont, West Virginia. Leadership, Vol. 17, no. 2.

- But it makes me happy. Doesn't God want me
to be happy?

The first lie may be small, but the combination of lies over time blinds, binds and destroys. Therefore, pray "Dear God, deliver me from Satan's destructive intent and his deceptive instruments. Free me from the smallest of his lies."

...FROM "THE EFFECTS OF EVIL"

Charles Haddon Spurgeon describes Satan encouraging a believer found drunk: "Do it again, do it again. For, the grief you feel about it now you will never feel any more if you commit the sin again."[44] Satan's binding lie is, "Keep sinning, for it will hurt worse if you stop." Yet, the reverse is true. The more you sin, the tighter you wrap yourself in the lie becoming more bound to the sin.

David's story, however, is different. Though tightly wrapped in his sin, David shows how, through prayer, you can be delivered. You can be set free.

David's Declining Path

2 Samuel 11 records David's declining path of sin. It begins in verse 1 with the sin of *irresponsibility*. In a season of war, David sends others to do his job. James 4:17 explains,

---

[44] Charles Haddon Spurgeon, *The Quotable Spurgeon* (Wheaton: Harold Shaw Publishers, Inc, 1990).

"So, for the person who knows to do good and doesn't do it, it is a sin."

David's sin declines further into poor *self-discipline*. In verse 2, he sees Bathsheba bathing. Instead of turning away, he stays to watch. A retired country preacher once said, "Men, if you are surprised by something you shouldn't see, you're not accountable for the first look if you turn away. But you are accountable for the second look if you turn back to see more."

David did not turn away. He stayed to see more causing his sin to decline to *disobedience* in verse 3. He sleeps with Bathsheba. She becomes pregnant and David's sin reaches bottom with *rebellion* instead of repentance. In verses 6–27, David has Bathsheba's husband killed in battle so he could marry Bathsheba and cover up his sin.

During a family vacation to the Smoky Mountains of Gatlinburg, Tennessee, I learned something about driving down steep mountains: It's not a straight road. You reach bottom taking one winding turn after another. David did not reach bottom immediately. He took four downward turns:

> David was where he shouldn't have been (vs. 1).
> David saw what he shouldn't have seen (vs. 2).
> David did what he shouldn't have done (vs. 3–5).
> David covered up what he should have confessed (vs. 6–27).

Yet God loved David enough not to leave him at the bottom. God teaches David how the journey back up begins with confrontation.

David's Delivering Prayer

In 2 Samuel 12, God sends His prophet Nathan to confront David about his sin. David mournfully replies in verse 13, *"I have sinned against the LORD."* He pens his prayer to God in Psalm 51. David's prayer models what to pray when praying for deliverance.

PRAYER OF CONFESSION

God confronts you with your sin anticipating a confession. David offers such a prayer in Psalm 51:3–4.

> *[3] For I am conscious of my rebellion,*
> *and my sin is always before me.*
> *[4] Against You—You alone— I have sinned*
> *and done this evil in your sight. ...*

David doesn't blame other people or circumstances. He takes full responsibility for his actions, saying it was *"my rebellion,"* *"my sin,"* *"I have sinned."* The first step of deliverance involves accepting responsibility for your sin and confessing it to God.

PRAYER FOR CLEANSING

Beyond admitting your sin (confession) is your plea for forgiveness (cleansing). David does this in verses 7–9:

> *[7] Purify me with hyssop, and I will be clean;*
> *wash me, and I will be whiter than snow.*

⁸ Let me hear joy and gladness;
let the bones you have crushed rejoice.
⁹ Turn your face away from my sins
and blot out all my guilt.

David paints a vivid picture when praying *"Purify me with hyssop."* When a leper cast from the community was miraculously healed, he went to the priest. After showing himself whole, a sacrifice was offered on his behalf using hyssop. When the ceremony ended, he resumed life back in the community.

David prays, "God, my confession has made me whole, but I need to know you have forgiven me and announced me clean." Only then David experiences the *"joy and gladness"* of resuming his life with God.

After our dachshund Oscar (named for Oscar Meyer Wieners) has his bath, the one drying him announces, "Look out! Here comes Oscar." The bathroom door opens and Oscar bolts from the room. He runs full speed to find everyone in the house. Playful as a puppy, he runs, jumps and turns as though to let everyone know "I'm clean."

That is how I picture David in his prayer for cleansing. Freed from the confines of his tightly-spun sin, he now dances before the Lord just as he did in 2 Samuel 6:14.

That is the initial feeling of deliverance. What you thought was hidden was confronted, confessed, and cleansed. Nothing remains between you and God. You are free from the bindings of your sin and free to resume your life with Him. Like David, you want to dance before God.

PRAYER FOR CREATING

Though deliverance begins with celebration, depression can follow. Reflecting on what you have done and considering all you have missed with God, remorse emerges. You sense it in David's third request. In verses 10–12, he prays for creating.

> *10 God, create a pure heart for me,*
> *and renew a steadfast spirit within me.*
> *11 Do not banish me from Your presence*
> *or take Your Holy Spirit from me.*
> *12 Restore the joy of Your salvation to me*
> *and give me a willing spirit.*

David asks God to create in him a *"pure heart."* This Hebrew word means to form something that did not exist. David's affections and passions were corrupted by Satan's lies. But, after confessing and cleansing, David wants God to fashion a new heart within him, a heart with pure and godly passions.

With a new heart, David also wants God to restore the joy of his salvation. As an older king, David says of God in Psalm 23:3, *"He restores my soul." (NKJV)* This word "restore" does not mean to recondition something damaged, but to restore it to its original condition. Thus, David asks God to give him a new heart, restoring his original relationship with God. What a great prayer. What a priceless gift.

In high school, my brother and I rented a 1965 Mustang from Dad. Though a classic, it was far from mint condition. Dad bought it and drove it home, sitting on a bucket (a literal bucket seat). He repaired it enough for my older brother and me to drive through high school. When it came time for each of us to go to college, we could have what he was driving or keep the Mustang. We both chose the newer car, thanking Dad for his sacrifice. Dad, however, was waiting for the Mustang.

After re-upholstering the seats and installing new carpet, he repainted the car its original misty blue. Project by project, Dad returned the car to its original condition. As a result, Dad was offered $11,000 in 1982 for a car he drove several hundred miles sitting on a bucket. Needless to say, my brother and I were sick.

Even after confession and cleansing, you may feel spiritually damaged. Yet, David proves that through prayer God takes you and restores you to the original condition He wanted for you. Out of Satan's hands and into God's, you once again feel valuable.

PRAYER OF SURRENDER

Praying for God's deliverance seeks more than freedom from sin. You petition God to serve again. David offers such a prayer in verse 13.

[13] Then I will teach the rebellious your ways, and sinners will return to you.

Too often, those bound by Satan and freed by God feel too ashamed to serve. Yet David held a different opinion. Having been wrapped in sin and freed by God, he was too grateful not to serve. He surrendered afresh his remaining years to God.

After his sin with Bathsheba, David lives another thirty years. Because of his renewed surrender, look at what God accomplishes through him.

- David overcomes the consequences of his sin—a national civil war.
- David provides the blueprints and provisions for God's temple.
- David mentors his son Solomon who leads Israel to its greatest years.
- David continues writing psalms to God that bless countless to this day.

David lives more grateful for God's deliverance than remorseful over his sin. That is why his prayer for deliverance is actually a prayer of surrender. Freed from his sin, David sees God use him again.

In 1919, Roy Regals of California picks up a Georgia Tech fumble and sprints for a touchdown. The only problem was, Regals ran the wrong way. His own teammate tackles him two yards from the wrong end zone, eventually giving Georgia Tech a two-point safety.

At halftime, Regals slumps at his locker with his face in his hands. Before resuming the second half, the coach orders,

"The starting team goes back onto the field to begin the second half." With the team gone Regals, still at his locker, wails, "I can't do it, Coach. I can't play. I've ruined the team." Unwavering, his coach barks, "Get up, Regals. The game is only half over. You belong on the field."[45]

Deceived by Satan's lies and snared by sin, we'd rather hide in the locker room. Shame and embarrassment does that. Yet God, the unwavering coach, says, "Get up. The game is only half over. You belong on the field." You may have pulled yourself from the game because of sin, but with confession, cleansing and creating, God frees you from sin. Now, He expects you back in the game. That is the prayer of surrender.

OCCASIONAL CHECK UPS

Years ago a boy walks into a drug store asking the pharmacist to use the phone. The pharmacist hears the boy say, "Hello, Dr. Anderson. Do you want a boy to cut the grass and run errands for you? … Oh, you already have a boy doing that and you are satisfied with him. OK, then. Goodbye." The pharmacist inquires, "Son, if you are looking for work, I could use a boy like you." "Thank you," the boy replied, "but I already have a job." "But weren't you trying to get a job from Dr. Anderson?" the pharmacist presses. "No, sir," the boy answers. "You see, I'm the boy who works for Dr. Anderson. I was just checking up on myself."[46]

[45] Steve May, *The Story File* (Peabody, Massachusetts: Hendrickson Publishers, 2000), 121.
[46] Ibid., 287.

The last petition in the Lord's Prayer provides a personal check-up. Praying "deliver me from the evil one" evaluates the following. First, do you still realize your need for deliverance? Through his lies, Satan wants to blind, bind, and destroy your salvation and service to God. Do you practice preventative praying? Are you asking God to help you detect and turn from Satan's lies before they snare you?

Second, if a sin traps you, are you willing to pray David's prayer of deliverance? Will you confess your sin and ask God to cleanse and restore you? Furthermore, will you surrender afresh to God and get back in the game with Him?

Third, are you in the game? Your deliverance is not complete until you are able to compete for your coach again. Are you in the game?

Chapter 9

MAKING
A PRAYER LIST

Sitting on his front porch in Kentucky waiting for his Social Security check, Harland wants more out of life. Making a list of the things he can still do, he pens, "Cooking Mom's recipe for fried chicken."

Asking local restaurant owners to add his chicken to their menu, Harland's chicken becomes the most popular item. Soon 600 different restaurants pay him 5 cents per chicken sold. Wishing to retire again, Harland sells his small franchise. The new owners, however, offer to pay Harland handsomely to promote the franchise. Harland "Colonel" Sanders agrees becoming the icon for his own Kentucky Fried Chicken.[47] It's a marvelous success story that began with making a list.

Like me, you may have a love-hate relationship with lists. You love what they do for you and hate what they do to you.

---

[47] Bruce Thielemann, "Dealing with Discouragement," *Preaching Today*, Tape No. 48.

You love how they help you see the day but hate becoming a slave to them. You love checking things off it, but hate adding more to it. Whether making lists on paper or electronically, lists are here to stay. Yet creating lists for everything else in life makes you resist doing so for your spiritual life. To strengthen your prayer life, consider making a prayer list.

WHY MAKE A PRAYER LIST

No verse says, "Thou shalt make a prayer list!" Still, there are multiple reasons and biblical references supporting the effort.

To Pray Specifically

One reason for making a prayer list is it helps you pray more specifically. Philippians 4:6 explains,

> *6 Don't worry about anything, but in everything, through prayer and petition with thanksgiving, let your requests be made known to God.*

The slogan "Worry about nothing. Pray about everything" comes from this verse.

There are twenty-six references to prayer in the book of Acts. All but four use the same Greek word in Philippians 4:6—*proseuchomai*. It refers to a specific request of God. In Philippians 4:6, your specific request surfaces from a specific need and becomes a "petition," meaning to ask out of need.

Therefore, you need to know your specific need in order to ask God's specific help.

I agree with Carol Gelderman: "Writing is the most exact form of thinking."[48] It helps you discern your need and shape your request. Furthermore, writing your prayers makes them more proactive than reactive. Doctors work to discern the disease over the symptoms. That enables them to prescribe specific medication for a specific disease. Writing out your prayers enables you to see the real need and pen a specific prayer request for it.

To Pray Persistently

Another benefit of a prayer list is it allows you to repeat your prayers. Luke's account of the Lord's Prayer emphasizes this.

Luke 11:1 opens with Jesus' disciples asking Him, "Lord, teach us to pray…." Jesus gives them the Lord's Prayer in verses 2–4. Then in verses 5–8, Jesus encourages them to pray persistently by telling the story of a man pounding continually on his neighbor's door until getting what he needs. Finally, in verses 9–10, Jesus ends the story with a command,

> [9] *"So I say to you, keep asking, and it will be given to you. Keep searching, and you will find. Keep knocking, and the door will be opened to you.* [10] *For everyone who asks receives, and the one who searches finds, and to the one who knocks, the door will be opened."*

---

[48] quoty.org/quote/4011.

Written as imperatives, Jesus commands you to keep on asking, seeking, and knocking. Not only are you to be specific in what you ask, but you are to ask persistently.

A prayer list helps you pray persistently because you can re-read it. If you do not understand instructions, re-read the manual. If you have forgotten the requirements, re-read the policy. When I forget what Loree sent me to the store to buy, I re-read the list. Furthermore, I use the list to check off what is in the basket and see what I still need.

Your prayer list allows you to keep praying for what remains unanswered. And if it remains unanswered for a long time, you can ask God if He wants you to ask Him differently. In his book, *The Doctrine of Prayer*, T.W. Hunt says God sometimes says no to our prayers because we are not asking for what He wants, or are not asking it the way He wants. Furthermore, your prayer list becomes a praise list when you see God answering your prayers.

To Pray Accurately

Kelly Kennard was having her morning devotion when the phone rang. Her three-year-old daughter Kayla answered. Kelly overheard her politely tell the caller, "My mom is having her 'emotions' now. Can she call you back?"[49]

When persistent specific prayers remain unanswered, you might call your morning devotions, "morning emotions." If

---

[49] Kelly Kennard, Willard, OH. Today's Christian Woman, "Heart to Heart."

so, your prayer list remains a vital tool, for if God has not answered your prayer, your request may not be in line with His will. 1 John 5:14–15 teaches,

> *[14] Now this is the confidence we have before Him: Whenever we ask anything according to His will, He hears us. [15] And if we know that He hears whatever we ask, we know that we have what we have asked Him for.*

Your prayer list allows you to review your requests and determine if they are in line with God's will. Furthermore, you can look at your prayer list and ask, "God, do you want to show me something better or teach me something deeper?" The Apostle Paul learns this when asking God three times to heal him and each time God says, "No." Finally, Paul gleans in 2 Corinthians 12:8–9,

> *[8] Concerning this, I pleaded with the Lord three times to take it away from me. [9] But He said to me, "My grace is sufficient for you, for power is perfected in weakness." Therefore, I will most gladly boast all the more about my weaknesses, so that Christ's power may reside in me.*

Making a prayer list allows you to evaluate requests that remain unanswered. Ask God if anything needs to change so you can pray for what He wants to do in and through you.

To Pray Effectively

When evaluating your prayer list, ask yourself, "How can these requests be more effective?" James 5:16 says, *"The prayer of a righteous man is powerful and effective."* (NIV)

In 1906, the Italian economist Vilfredo Pareto discovered that 20% of the Italian people owned 80% of the country's wealth. Since his discovery, his 80–20 rule appears in other areas as the Pareto Principle.[50] When applied to time management, it means that 20% of your priorities yield 80% of your production. Therefore, devote your time to what's most important.

If the Pareto Principle were applied to prayer, it means that 20% of your requests yield 80% of your answers. It encourages you to evaluate your requests and pray for what is most important.

After teaching His Lord's Prayer in Matthew 6, Jesus instructs us in verses 31–33 to evaluate and prioritize our prayers:

> [31] *"So don't worry, saying, 'What will we eat?' or 'What will we drink?' or 'What will we wear?'* [32] *For the idolaters eagerly seek all these things, and your heavenly Father knows that you need them.* [33] *But seek first the kingdom of*

---

[50] Arthur W. Hafner, "Pareto's Principle: 80-20 Rule", http://www.public.asu.edu/~dmuthua/pareto's_principle.html.

God and His righteousness, and all these things will be provided for you."

Making a prayer list keeps you from praying for what's unimportant and unproductive. It focuses your attention on kingdom requests, which provide answers to other needs as well. For example, praying for a boss's salvation also answers your prayer for a better work environment.

To Pray Measurably

A final reason for making a prayer list comes from David's life. David's story reads more like a novel than a biography. He's the shepherd boy, secretly anointed king, who later kills Goliath. He's the young general women sing about who lives as a fugitive from his King. When finally crowned king, David unites the people only to divide them because of his adultery. Later, he rallies them to give for the building of the temple.

David's psalms read as his prayer journal. God inspires David to write over seventy psalms. Fourteen of them draw from historic experiences in his life. The others cascade from his life with God. Therefore, to measure David's walk with God, read his psalms. If you want to measure your walk with God, read your prayer lists.

The following example comes from my prayer journal. Sadly, it shows I had not written a prayer list in three months. It reveals, however, the greatness of God and the importance of writing and praying through a prayer list.

Dear Heavenly Father,

I have been fearful to start praying and writing again. I'm frightened that I'm so overwhelmed I wouldn't know where to start, and if I did start, I'd never stop. Yet reflecting on the prayer in December, I see how You have already answered many of my prayers. Therefore, by faith, I trust You will answer these as well.

Here's a list as they come to mind. (My prayer list filled three pages. Here are a few):

- *Lord, Please call out Sunday school workers to be trained and ready to serve and minister by September 2nd. We will need seventy.*

- *Father, I need to find the Minister of Youth you plan to have here, and I'd like to have him here by July 8th.*

- *I also need the secretary you have planned for me to start April 16th. Please, help me not be impatient so as to miss who you have planned. Yet help me see her and please send her soon.*

Father, I'll stop now and will pray these through. Please know I love you and will work at making time with you a priority of my life.

Now move forward almost four months and listen to the following entry.

Dear Father,

> *As I read through March's prayer letter, I am humbled by your answers. We needed more Sunday school workers and over fifty came forward. We are calling a Minister of Youth. This was confirmed on the phone July 8th. Furthermore, I now have a secretary who is a blessing. Through these answers you remind me of your power and presence. You invite me and encourage me to continue to pray. Therefore, I pray... (I wrote another prayer list that filled two pages.)*

The beauty of a prayer list is it not only measures your walk with God, but also measures God's work through you. You have a running ledger of the great deposits of God in your life through prayer. Furthermore, your answered prayers become your list of reasons for making more prayer lists and continuing to pray.

MAKING A "LORD'S PRAYER" LIST

By now, you understand the benefits of making a prayer list. However, if you have never written a prayer list, where do you begin? Begin with the best. And, the best model for a prayer list is the Lord's Prayer. Teaching His disciples how to pray in Matthew 6:9–13, Jesus said,

> ⁹ *"Therefore, you should pray like this:*
> *"'Our Father in heaven,*
> *Your name be honored as holy.*
> ¹⁰ *Your kingdom come.*
> *Your will be done*
> *on earth as it is in heaven.*
> ¹¹ *Give us today our daily bread.*
> ¹² *And forgive us our debts,*
> *as we also have forgiven our debtors.*
> ¹³ *And do not bring us into temptation,*
> *but deliver us from the evil one.'"*

Jesus did not need to motivate His followers to pray. The Jews already prayed three times a day, which is more than many Christians. Praying their Salat five times a day, Moslems pray more than most. Obviously, Christians need to be motivated to pray. However, Jesus' purpose of the Lord's Prayer was not motivation but modeling how to pray. Motivation comes through praying like Jesus. According to Jesus' model, your prayer list has five sections.

Picturing God

When Jesus prays, *"Our Father in heaven, Your name be honored as holy,"* He encourages you to see God as your loving Father, powerful King, and holy Lord before making a request. Beginning with a big picture of God gives you a clear picture in prayer. Therefore, to start with the right picture of God, let me suggest

- Praising God by name—*The names of God mentioned in scripture refer to His deeds and character. As you say them, you see Him and praise Him.*[51]
- Praising God for His faithfulness—*Recall how God has provided for, protected, and guided you. Don't overlook your salvation as a key example of His faithfulness.*
- Praising God with scripture—*Scripture records how others have praised Him. Read their praises as an example and inspiration.*[52]
- Praising God in song—*Over seventy times the psalms encourage us to sing to the Lord. It happens naturally. After you praise God by name and with scripture, your heart overflows with song.*

---

[51] Two helpful works on praying the names of God are Tony Evans, *Praying Through the Names of God (Eugene, Oregon: Harvest House, 2014)*, and Tony Evans, *The Power of the Names of God (Eugene, Oregon: Harvest House, 2014)*. The former is a devotional guide aiding you as you pray through more than 80 names of God found in scripture. The later is a deeper study regarding fifteen of the names of God in scripture.

[52] The Psalms are layered with worship pieces to God. You'll also find meaningful praises of God in Isaiah, and moving descriptions of worship in heaven in Revelation 4,5,20,21.

Opening prayer with the right picture of God is an act of worship. It shapes what you ask Him.

God's Kingdom and Will

Before rushing to God with a list of wants, picturing God causes you to ask, "God, what do you want?" Jesus models this when praying, *"Your kingdom come. Your will be done."* To help discern what God wants, ask yourself:

- What will grow God's kingdom within me and through me?
- How do I ask God's help in knowing His will?
- What is God asking me to do to fulfill His will and reveal His glory?

Here is where the Pareto Principle proves itself in prayer. Giving priority to requests that spread God's kingdom and fulfill His will reveals other needs as well (Matthew 6:33). Do not forget to use Jesus' example in John 17. (We covered it in chapter four.)

Your Day

As a loving Father, God wants to hear what you need. 1 Peter 5:7 bids us, *"casting all your care upon Him because he cares about you."* Jesus says you are to pray, *"Give us today our daily bread."* Remember, "bread" refers to your needs, not wants, and "daily" means focusing on today and trusting

God for tomorrow. Therefore, here are some pointers when praying for your day.

- What is my schedule for the day and are there any concerns?
- What do I need from God to honor Him during the day?

These two questions bring to mind the practice of supply and demand. Tell God the demands of your day before you start. Trust Him to supply your needs as you go (2 Corinthians 9:8). This gives you the confidence you need to fulfill God's will and reveal His glory throughout the day.

Your Relationships

Life would be easier if the supply and demand of each day were purely material and never relational. Yet most daily demands emerge from relationships. Jesus experienced it. Of the sixteen chapters in Mark's Gospel, there are only two chapters Jesus is not meeting a need.

Realizing the importance of maintaining godly relationships, Jesus teaches you to pray, *"Forgive us our debts, as we also have forgiven our debtors."* With the image of debt in mind, ask yourself:

- What do I owe God in order to have a right relationship with Him?

- What do I owe my spouse, children, parents or others to have a godly relationship with them?

The weight of financial debt is heavy until settled. Likewise, the burden of relational debt weighs you down until settled with God and others. But once settled, you enjoy the freedom of living debt free.

God's Protection

Satan deceives to blur your perspective and skew your priorities. He causes you to doubt God's help straining your relationships with God and others. That is why Jesus commands you to pray, *"And do not bring us into temptation, but deliver us from the evil one."* This is an important part of your prayer. Therefore, let me recommend praying:

- Father, help me be aware of subtle temptations (1 Peter 5:8)
- Lord, help me resist the following temptations (James 4:7)
- God, set me free from these chronic temptations (1 Corinthians 10:13)

Jesus was God in flesh. He taught His model prayer after Satan tempted Him in the wilderness. That is why praying for God's protection is a mandatory part of every believer's prayer list. If Satan would tempt Jesus, you know he will tempt you.

MAKING A DIFFERENCE

Colonel Harland Sanders sold his Kentucky Fried Chicken franchise for 2 million dollars in 1964. In 1986, PepsiCo Inc. bought the franchise from RJR Nabisco for 840 million dollars. Today, Kentucky Fried Chicken is part of the world's largest restaurant company with over 32,500 units in more than 100 countries and territories.[53] All of this began when Harland wrote a list of all the things *HE COULD DO*.

Consider the difference God can make in and through you when you make a prayer list that involves praying...

With a picture of God...
for God's kingdom and will...
for your relationships...
and for God's protection.

Unlike Colonel Sanders, your list is not based on what you can do. Your prayer list is based on what *GOD CAN DO THROUGH YOU*, and God does far more than cook chicken.

---

[53] "About KFC: Colonel Harland Sanders," http://www.kfc.com/about/colonel.htm